"...I WILL BUILD
MY CHURCH"

"... I WILL BUILD MY CHURCH"

CENTENNIAL EDITION

"...I WILL BUILD MY CHURCH"

by THEA B. VAN HALSEMA

Illustrated by DIRK GRINGHUIS

GRAND RAPIDS
INTERNATIONAL PUBLICATIONS
Distributed by Kregel's, Grand Rapids, Mich.

Set up and lithoprinted
in the United States of America
by Feature Publishing Service,
Grand Rapids, Michigan

151 0

TO DICK

BECAUSE HE HAS HELPED ME TO
LOVE BETTER THE WHOLE OF CHRIST'S
CHURCH ON EARTH, AND THAT PART
OF IT CALLED CHRISTIAN REFORMED.

THE CHAPTERS

"...I WILL BUILD MY CHURCH"

FOUR PAPERS

Twenty men in Sunday black suits were in the church. It was a small church, made of logs. Eighteen of the men sat in the straight wood benches of the church. They sat together, in the front near the pulpit. One man stood up, facing the men in the benches. The other man sat at a table with a quill pen in his hand and a stack of papers before him.

The twenty men wore their Sunday black suits, but it was not Sunday. Wednesday it was, an April Wednesday. The men were ministers and elders from nine churches. They had traveled over muddy spring roads in their horsedrawn carriages to the log church in the town of Zeeland for an all-day meeting. It was an important meeting, a meeting of the classis. Twice a year the men met as a classis to decide the affairs of the churches, the churches in western Michigan which called themselves Reformed.

The man with the quill pen dipped it in the ink. *April 8, 1857,* he wrote on the top of a clean sheet of paper. On the second line he added, *Meeting held in the church building of Zeeland.* But he did not write exactly those words. Instead he wrote in his own language, the language of all the men in the church. He wrote the words in Dutch.

The man standing up was in charge of the meeting. He was a minister, and president for the day. First he preached a sermon and then he prayed. After the prayer he began to conduct the business of the churches.

The men met together all morning and when lunch was over they took their places in the church again. First they stood to pray. When they sat down, the president nodded to the man at the table, who was the secretary. The secretary picked up four papers from the pile on his table and began to read from them. As he read, the men became very still in their benches.

What did they say, these four papers? And where did they come from?

They came from four places. One came from a city. The city was new and growing. It sprang up beside a river where the water tumbled down over rocks to make a rapids. So people had called the city Grand Rapids. Among the churches in Grand Rapids was the Second Dutch Reformed Church. From the minister of this church came one of the papers. On it he had written in a letter what he and many of his people believed.

The other papers came from three churches in the country. They were log churches like the church in Zeeland, and they stood among tall trees which were old and cornfields which were new. In each church there was a wood stove for heating, and near the door a pail of water hanging with a tin dipper for people who became thirsty. Around each country church there were a few houses. Beyond the houses were the green fields. And beyond the fields were the forests which the men had moved back with their axes to make room for the fields.

There was one paper from the country church of Noordeloos. The minister had written it. And another paper from the church of Graafschap. The last came from the church at Polkton, the place called Coopersville today. The elders had written these, because their churches did not have ministers.

The four papers came from different places, but they said the same thing. They said it in the language of a land across the sea. Though the words of each were different, the meaning was the same.

We will no longer be a part of you, said the four letters to the classis. *You have joined a group of churches in this land and taken their name. We cannot be a part of them with you, for they do not live and worship as we believe God wants us to do.*

And so we will be by ourselves, as you were too when first we settled here together. We will be a church by ourselves with a name of our own in this new country which we crossed an ocean to find. The Lord open your eyes that you may stand with us. O brothers in Christ, walk again with us in the way of our fathers.

A church and a name of our own, said the papers. A new church in a new land. Where is this church today? What has happened to it during the years since it began?

This has happened: In the place of the four churches there are five hundred. They stretch from Alaska to Florida, from Nova Scotia to California. They send missionaries even farther, to the other side of the world. Much has happened since the day when the four papers lay on the table in the log church of Zeeland. And God has done it all. He has done great things for the church which is called Christian Reformed.

THE TREE OF THE CHURCH

A hundred years — does that seem like a long time to you? Then you will be surprised to know that the story of the Christian Reformed Church really begins much earlier. It begins not one hundred but nineteen hundred years ago. It begins not in the log church of Zeeland, but in the winding streets of old Jerusalem. It begins not on an April Wednesday in 1857 but on a busy Jewish feast day called Pentecost in the year 30 after Christ. Our story begins then because that was the beginning of the church of Jesus Christ. The Christian Reformed Church is a part of this great church.

You see, the church of Jesus is somewhat like a tree. It has many branches. Some branches are large and very old. Newer branches have come from them. Some branches are strong and full of life. Others have become dead. These dead branches are the churches which no longer preach the truth about Jesus, and so they can no longer be part of his true church.

The Christian Reformed Church is one of the newer branches of the tree. It is only about a hundred years old although the tree began to grow nineteen hundred years ago. So before we tell the story of our branch, we want to know about the rest of the tree from which it grew.

A CROSS IN THE SUNSET

The very first church after Jesus went to heaven was the church in Jerusalem. It did not have a building, but it had people who believed in God's Son, and this is all that matters. The disciples were in this church and so were a small group of other believers. But the Jews who had killed Jesus were in Jerusalem, too. They hunted everywhere to find the believers, and they killed them or put them in jail. In the streets of Jerusalem people were telling each other that the new Jesus religion would not last.

16

To escape from this persecution, believers fled from Jerusalem to other cities. Wherever they made their new homes, they talked to others about Jesus. Many people believed. New churches were begun in homes where groups of believers began to meet together. And so God used the sword of persecution to send the good news of Jesus on its first important march into new places. It spread from one city, Jerusalem, to many more.

In one of these places, a seaport called Antioch, the people of the town began to call the believers "Christians." Christians, meaning *of Christ.* Down through the years that name has been used. We have it as the first word in the name of our church, Christian Reformed.

Many more churches were begun by the apostles and other missionaries who walked miles and miles to preach from town to town. Everywhere the Holy Spirit opened people's hearts to believe. They began to live and worship as Christians. Nothing could stop the gospel as it spread like wildfire in the lands around the Mediterranean Sea.

But it did not spread without meeting strong enemies. Jews in many cities were the first enemies of the church, but Gentiles did not like the new religion either. For years the Gentiles had been worshiping hundreds of idol gods. Then along came this new religion called Christianity whose god could not even be seen. Yet it claimed to be the only religion and to worship the only true God. The Gentiles would not give up their many gods for a god who said he was the only one. They tried to stop this new religion from coming to their cities.

During the first three hundred years of the church, Christians suffered in many places. The emperor Nero, who was so cruel he had his own mother killed, tortured the Christians in Rome. He invited the whole city to watch. Some Christians he killed by turning hungry lions and leopards loose to eat them. Others

17

were tied in the skins of animals to be torn apart by wild dogs. Some Christians were dragged and gored by angry bulls. Others were hung on crosses which stood in the sand of the amphitheater floor. Sometimes Nero gave evening garden parties which he lighted by tying Christians to piles of wood and burning them to amuse himself and his guests.

In the year 303 after Christ there came to the throne of the Roman Empire a man named Diocletian. Diocletian announced that he would wipe out Christianity, the religion of Jesus Christ. He was so sure he could do it that he had a new coin made. On it was a picture of himself and these words, "Diocletian, the emperor who destroyed the Christian name."

Now Christians suffered everywhere. Throughout the Roman world, soldiers of the emperor went into action. Throughout the Roman world, Christians hid themselves. For ten terrible years the persecution reached to every corner of the empire, killing Christians everywhere.

In Rome the Christians hid in miles of twisting underground passageways called catacombs. These tunnels and rooms had been dug to bury the bodies of dead people. Can you imagine that the catacombs would have stretched five hundred miles if they had been laid in a straight line?

Here the Christians of Rome hid and worshiped. By the light of torches they sang and listened to preaching. Sometimes they ate the bread and wine of the Lord's Supper together. If they dared, they crept back to their homes during the night. Many stayed underground for months, and even here the soldiers sometimes found them.

Then suddenly all persecution stopped. God stopped it in a surprising way. Two men were preparing to fight each other to see which would be the next emperor. Each had a large army. One of them, a man named Constantine, thought he saw a cross shining in the sunset the evening before the battle. Being a superstitious man, he decided to fight in the name of this sign. When he won the battle, he believed the cross had done it for him. So he rewarded the religion of the cross by ordering all persecution of Christians stopped, and he made Christianity equal to every other religion. This order of Constantine is called the Edict of Milan and he made it in the year 313 after Christ.

In this sign, conquer...

How triumphantly the church of Christ came through its first three hundred years! Never since has it grown as fast as it did then. From one suffering little church it had grown until hundreds of churches were spread throughout the world of that time. The Jews could not stop the church in Jerusalem. Fierce persecutions could not stop it in the whole Roman Empire. God was blessing his church, and nothing on earth could stop it.

THE CHURCH CHANGES

Overnight, the Christians were free, free to live and work and worship. They came out of their hiding places into a place of honor. Before ten years had passed, Constantine made the Christian religion the official religion of the whole empire. He gave large gifts of money and land to the church and had beautiful church buildings built. By his order Sunday became a day of rest from work because it was the Christian holy day.

During the three hundred years when the Christians had been hated and killed, they had had to love Jesus enough to die for him. And so only people who loved Christ with all their hearts wanted to be members of his church. This had made the church strong and pure.

It is easy to guess what happened when Constantine made Christianity the religion of the empire. Suddenly everyone wanted to join the Christian church, not because they truly loved Jesus as the people did who were ready to die for him, but because it was popular and good style to be a Christian. No doubt some of the new members learned to know Jesus as their Savior, but many of them flocked to the church only because they wanted to be like everyone else and please the emperor.

Things began to change in the church. Some changes were good, but other changes began to lead the church farther away from what God wanted it to be.

It was good that the church could send out missionaries again. The missionaries set out to convert the chiefs and their tribes of uncivilized people who lived in the north of Europe.

Patrick was the first missionary to Ireland. He was born in Scotland but some Irish pirates caught him when he was sixteen. They sold him as a slave to a chief in North Ireland, but Patrick escaped on a ship to France and Italy where he studied to become a priest. Here he dreamed he heard voices from the coast of Ireland. "We beseech thee, child of God, come and walk again among us," called the voices. Patrick went back bravely and began preaching in the open fields. By the time he died, he had established more than three hundred churches.

Augustine and thirty other missionaries went together to England. They were sent by Gregory, head of the church, after he had seen some blonde blue-eyed boys being sold in the slave market of Rome. Gregory asked about these light-colored boys and someone told him they were Angles, brought from England. "They look more like angels," said Gregory and decided to send missionaries to their country. Augustine and his men almost turned back because the Angles were so fierce. But they found a kind chief whose wife had learned about Christ in the land where she was born. Soon this king and many of his people accepted the Christian religion. One Christmas day Augustine baptized ten thousand people by sprinkling water on them from a hyssop branch.

Boniface was the great missionary to the dark forests of Germany. He once gathered a crowd of pagan people together in a village where a huge oak tree stood. The tree was worshiped as holy to Thor, the god of thunder. Boniface said he would cut down

the tree to prove that Thor was not the true god. The people were afraid as he cut it down, but when nothing happened, many of them accepted the Christian religion and were baptized. From the wood of the tree, Boniface began the building of a church.

In the Netherlands, too, where many of our grandparents were born, wild tribes once lived. When the missionary Willibrod and twelve others went to see Radbod, king of Friesland, he sacrificed one of them to his false gods. Boniface went to the Netherlands as an old man after he had worked many years in Germany. In the town of Dokkum, some pagan men hid one night while Boniface was meeting with a group of new Christians. The men attacked him with clubs and Boniface fell, holding above his head copies of the gospels. This great missionary and fifty Christians with him were clubbed to death.

While the missionaries preached to faraway tribes, the church at home was changing. Its buildings became grand and beautiful, made from special stone with costly furnishings. The altar stood in the middle at the front of the church, and the pulpit for preaching was moved off to the side. The ministers, now called priests, dressed in expensive robes and spent most of their time during the services at the altar instead of in the pulpit. The Lord's Supper began to look like a heathen sacrifice, blessed by the priests and passed out from the altar. People no longer sang their praise to God. Instead the priest and a well-trained choir chanted in Latin. Church worship began to look like a fancy pageant. The simple sincere worship of the early Christian church had disappeared.

Idols crept into the church, too. People had been so used to gods they could see that they took this custom along with them when they flocked into the Christian church. Images of Christ and Mary and the apostles were made, and people began to worship them. They burned candles and incense to them, just as they had done to their idol gods.

24

We know that Christ himself is the head of the church on earth. But during this time a man began to be called the leader of the church. He was the bishop of the important church in Rome. After the apostles died, the churches looked more and more to the bishop of Rome to settle their problems. He became powerful and called himself "papa." From this Latin word, which means father, comes the name pope. Soon the pope was in charge of churches everywhere.

Of course each pope in Rome was happy to be the head of the church. He wanted to be sure it stayed that way. One after another, the popes began to build up their power. They claimed that Peter had been the first bishop of Rome. So, they said, since Jesus made Peter chief of the apostles, the bishop of Rome should be chief of all the bishops.

But the bishop of the five-million-dollar church in Constantinople was not pleased that the pope of Rome was head of the church. He wished that he were. Constantinople is in the country now called Turkey on the eastern end of the Mediterranean Sea. The people of the lands in this eastern part spoke a different language and lived differently from the people in the western part who were part of Europe and nearer to Rome. After a while it became hard for the two groups to work together.

In 1054 there was a quarrel between the pope in Rome and the bishop in Constantinople. The pope ordered the bishop and his people put out of the church of Rome. The bishop answered by telling the pope he and his western people were put out of the church of Constantinople.

This is how it happened that the church around the Mediterranean Sea was divided into two parts a thousand years after Pentecost. Constantinople was the seat of the Greek eastern part, while the pope in Rome ruled the Latin western part.

25

AUGUSTINE WRITES OF SIN AND GRACE

There is one great churchman of these years whom we must not forget. His name was Augustine and he grew up in the splendid cities of North Africa. No one guessed when Augustine was young that he would ever be of any use to the Christian church. His mother Monica taught him about Jesus, but Augustine was not much interested.

He became an excellent student when he went to high school, but he also began to live wickedly. After he had become a teacher, Augustine left North Africa to go to Italy. He was restless and hoped to find some new learning that would make him happy. Monica stayed behind, praying for the soul of her son. In the city of Milan, Augustine went to hear Bishop Ambrose preach. At first he went because he admired the fine speaking of Ambrose, but slowly the gospel which Ambrose preached also began to mean something to Augustine. He had studied every other kind of belief without finding peace, and he was still miserable about his sinful life.

Then God through Christ gave peace to Augustine, forgiving his sins and making him a new man. And God also gave an answer to the endless prayers of Monica, Augustine's praying mother.

From that time, when he was thirty-three years old, until he died when he was seventy-six, Augustine studied and wrote and spoke and preached for God. He sold whatever he had inherited from his father and gave the money to the poor. With a few friends Augustine lived in a house which he later turned into a seminary to train new ministers. When he died, Augustine left behind a great treasury of writing from his brilliant mind. Especially he wrote on what the Bible tells us of sin and of God's grace. The church of all times speaks of Augustine's writings as next to those of Paul and equal to what John Calvin wrote a thousand years later.

A CHURCH SINKS INTO SIN

How would you like to live on the top of a pillar sixty feet high? In the land of Syria a man named Simon lived this way for thirty-seven years. The top of the pillar was only four feet square, a little bigger than a kitchen table. There was a railing around the top, and Simon often slept leaning against it. In sun and wind and rain he stayed on his pillar, pulling up food on a rope once a day.

Why did Simon live this way? Why didn't he live in a house with a family and go to church on Sundays as other Christians did? If we had asked Simon, he would have told us that he was not happy with some things in the Christian church. Living on a pillar was Simon's answer to these. Maybe it was not a good answer, but Simon was right about what was happening in the church. And what was happening?

The church was slowly slipping farther and farther away from what Christ wanted it to be. The slipping began after Constantine made Christianity the religion of the empire. By the time it ended, twelve hundred years later, the church of Christ hardly looked like a church anymore. It had become so full of sin that only a complete shakeup would make it ready to do the Lord's work again.

By what he did, Constantine tied the church and the state together as they never should be tied. The church began to get mixed up in the work of the government. It wanted to say who should be kings and how they should rule. The kings and princes wanted to tell the church who should be pope and who should be his chief bishops in every country. After a while the church and state were fighting together to see who was stronger.

For hundreds of years the church, through the pope, was the stronger. Popes said they stood halfway between God and man, below God but above man. They had no armies but they made people believe they had power to keep them out of heaven and send them to hell if they did not obey the church. Even kings came to beg forgiveness from the pope and agreed to obey him in all things. In the year 1077 Emperor Henry IV, the mightiest king of his day, stood barefoot in the snow at the gate of a castle to which he had come to beg forgiveness from the pope who was inside. For three days he stood in a rough wool shirt at the closed gate of the castle before the pope let him come in to kiss his feet and say he had done wrong.

28

The church grew rich. It collected property and gold and precious stones and heavy taxes from much of Europe. It quite forgot that its real treasure should have been laid up in heaven. The pope became the richest of all. One pope, when he died, left behind eighteen million gold florins in money and seven million in gold plate and jewels. While the poor people starved and begged, the popes became millionaires.

For a long time the pope allowed each king to appoint the church officials in his own land. The kings appointed their friends, because bishops lived like rich men and paid no taxes on their church property. And this is how the leaders of the Christian church began to be men who loved money more than God, men who had little desire to do God's work on earth.

In the Vatican, that part of Rome where the pope lived, some officials of the church spent their time gambling and drinking and living wickedly. Such things were going on among church rulers, who were supposed to teach and rule all the common members of the church. The leadership of the church on earth had become rotten indeed.

Not only did the church leaders live wickedly. They taught the people to believe much that was against what the Bible teaches. This was the worst sin of all.

The church taught its members that the pope could speak for God, and that everything the pope said was right and free from sin. This made the pope a kind of god and put his word above the word of God which he has given us in the Bible. In fact, popes ordered people not to read the Bible and said that only they and councils of the church could explain it. The people learned to pray to the pope and Mary and others who were called saints. The saints are holy, they were told, and can hear your prayers and answer them for God.

The church also taught its people that they had to do part of the paying for their sins. Besides what Christ did on the cross, each Christian must help to get himself to heaven, said the church. If he does not obey the church he will not go to heaven. Even after he dies his soul must stay a while in a halfway place called purgatory until it is good enough to go on to heaven. If his family on earth will say many prayers and burn candles to the saints in his name, his soul will get out of purgatory sooner.

The church had a long list of punishments for each sin. People confessed their sins to the priest every week and he told them what they had to do to make up for them.

When the church wanted to become richer, it found another way to make people pay for their sins. Pay with money, said the church. The people found this way quicker and easier, and the church was delighted to get the money. This evil plan was called the system of indulgences. People lined up to pay for their sins with money and received a piece of paper saying that the pope had ordered their sin forgiven. This they took to their priest to show that they had already paid for their sins.

No wonder the church did not want its members to read the Bible for themselves. Almost every page of that precious book tells us that Jesus paid once and for all for our sins when he died upon the cross. There were still people in the church who believed this truth. When they spoke against what the church was doing, do you know what the church often did to them? It killed them. It called them heretics for daring to speak against the church of Rome, and it burned them. Now the church itself was persecuting and killing people who believed what the Bible said.

We remember especially two men who spoke boldly against the sins of the church. One of them was a college professor in England named John Wycliffe. He told the people that the Bible, not the church, was the authority in their lives. Then he translated the Bible into the English language so that the people in his country could read it for themselves. The pope wanted to get his hands on Wycliffe but the English nobles protected him. Forty years after he died, a council of the church ordered his books burned and his bones dug up to be burned, too.

In the land of Bohemia, now Czechoslovakia, lived a man named John Huss. He was head of the seminary at the University of

Prague and he heard Wycliffe's teachings gladly. In his classes
and in his preaching, Huss spoke against indulgences and taught
the truths of the Bible. The people of Bohemia were becoming
dissatisfied with the church, and most of them began to side with
Huss. Eight months Huss was kept in prison after the pope had
him arrested. Then, after a pretense of a trial, he was brought
out to be burned. One by one his priest's clothes were taken off
him and he was cursed. A paper cap with three devils painted
on it was put on his head and he was burned to death. But the
burning of Huss did not stop the truths he had preached. They
only burned more brightly in the hearts of the people who had
heard him.

Other men too tried to preach and work against the evils of the church. But they could not break the power of the pope and his helpers. After twelve hundred years of sinking into sin, the church of Rome could not be changed from within. The mighty hand of God would reach down to shake out of the old church a new church fit to do his work on earth.

And the hand of God was moving.

It moved among the nations. It made them stronger, more able to stand against the pope. Kings and their people were no longer interested in obeying and paying for a faraway church and pope.

God moved in the hearts of people. Many of them became restless against the orders of the church and doubtful of what it taught them. Then came the great longing for learning, which was called the Renaissance. People began to think. They wanted to read and learn for themselves.

In Germany, God guided the hand of Johann Gutenberg, who invented printing with movable type. Now the Bible could be printed instead of handcopied and every man could own one to read for himself.

God chose leaders from among the people. A handful of leaders, each with a mind and a voice and a courage to do the work of the Lord.

Everywhere the hand of God moved. God was ready to reform his church, and not even the mighty church of Rome could stand against him.

"I CAN DO NO OTHERWISE"

Through the son of a German iron miner, God struck the first great blow at the sins of the church. Many people were waiting for that blow.

The miner's son was named Martin, because he was baptized on a cold November day when the church celebrated a day holy to Saint Martin, an early pope. The boy's family name was Luther, and his parents loved him well because he was their first child. They taught him the commandments and they took him through the narrow twisting streets of the town to the church where he saw the priest at the altar and heard the Latin chanting he could not understand.

In the shadows of the forest outside the town Martin gathered firewood with his mother. He listened when she told him of the little devils and spirits that hid about, hoping to do him evil and capture his soul. Every night he prayed to the saints to preserve him when he sinned against the holy God. When he lay in bed he pulled up the covers tightly and shivered to think that the devils in the wind and darkness might be stretching out their fingers after him.

Later Martin went to the university to study law. He passed with high honors the first course and then the masters' course. But he had not stopped worrying about his soul. For his father's sake he studied law, but for his own sake he wished to be sure his soul was saved, to know certainly that he was at peace with the almighty God.

One evening as Martin was walking back to the university after a visit at home, he made a vow that had been in his mind a long time. A storm came up, full of thunder and lightnings. God is angry, thought Martin, and he hurried to reach the next town.

Suddenly a lightning bolt struck close to him, so close that Martin thought he would be hit. God is angry with me, he told himself in terror. Falling flat on the wet earth, he cried out in the roar of thunder that followed the lightning flash, Save me, Saint Anne, and I will become a monk.

When the heavy door of the monastery swung shut behind Martin Luther, he left behind him an angry father and a crowd of surprised friends. But Martin entered eagerly. Here, he thought, in the arms of the church, I can find peace with God and pay for the load of my sins.

Brother Martin, they called the new monk. He was a good monk, too, working and praying and confessing his sins. But he did not find the peace he wanted. He did not even find it when he made the long trip walking over the mountains to Rome, the holy city.

There was a handcopied Latin Bible in the monastery. Brother Martin was always reading it. While his candle burned low beside the pages he read on, as if he were hunting for something. Often he read in the books of Paul. From cover to cover he studied the book which had been lost to him until then.

Here, in the words of God himself, Brother Martin found his peace. "The just shall live by faith," said God. "For by faith are ye saved, and not by works," said God in another place. Not through the church or the words of the church, not through any works of men, but straight through Jesus Christ, and by faith alone. So said God. Here was peace, sure peace.

It was while Luther was teaching in the University of Wittenberg that a monk named John Tetzel came to Germany to sell indulgences. The pope needed money for a new church in Rome, so he sent out indulgence salesmen to get it.

35

Tetzel arrived in each city with a big parade. Trumpets blew and heralds carried the silk flag of the pope at the head of the procession. The people followed close behind to the center of the town where Tetzel's helpers made ready to do business. They set down the big iron padlocked chest to receive the people's money. They laid ready the little pieces of paper which said, in the name of the pope, their sins were forgiven. Behind the table Tetzel stood on a platform and told the people how the souls of their dead fathers and mothers were crying in purgatory, waiting to be sent on to heaven. Pay for these and for your own sins, he shouted. "As soon as the coin in the coffer rings, the soul from purgatory springs."

The people were afraid when they heard Tetzel. They took their bread money and their savings and paid to get rid of the fear.

Martin Luther had been watching the wicked business Tetzel was doing from town to town. He knew he had to speak against it. On the last day of October in the year 1517, Luther walked through the streets to the Castle Church of Wittenberg, where he nailed on the wooden church doors his answer to indulgences. It was a long answer written in Latin, the language of the church. There were ninety-five sentences, or theses, and below them Luther wrote his offer to debate the theses with anyone at a public meeting.

Students read the long Latin sheet and passed the exciting news around. Then brave printers took up the news. Translated into the German language, Luther's theses found their way all over Germany.

Soon the indulgences did not sell very well. People kept their money. They had heard from the lips of a learned Bible professor what they had often wondered about in their own hearts.

Martin
Luther

Luther did not mean to fight the church and the pope when he nailed up his ninety-five theses. He meant only to stop the sale of indulgences in Germany and he hoped the church would listen to his arguments. At first the pope paid no attention. Some drunken monk, he said with a wave of his hand. But the news that came over the mountains did not please him. All Germany is with Luther, said the messengers who had been sent to investigate.

The pope struck back at the Wittenberg professor. Luther was put out of the church and copies of all his writings were burned at a public bonfire. If Prince Frederick, ruler of Saxony where Luther lived, had not been friendly to him, Luther would have been killed. Instead God kept him free twenty-five years longer, to write and preach to the people of Germany who heard him gladly.

In 1521 Luther was called to appear before the new emperor who was ruler over a large part of Europe. He had called all his princes to a meeting, known as a diet, in the city of Worms. A herald was sent to ride before the cart of Luther with the royal flag. Along the roads and in the villages through which Luther passed, the people gathered to wish him well. They were worried about what the emperor would do to their new leader. As the cart came to Worms, the watchman in the tower blew his horn to announce Luther's coming. People crowded into the street and hung from their windows to see him. Friends went in and out of his room all night.

The next day Martin Luther stood in the palace hall, one plain man before the powerful rulers of his day. The hall was packed with splendidly dressed princes. On a raised platform sat the new young emperor, who had pledged to defend the church of Rome until his death. Luther felt the unfriendly eyes upon him. He saw the power, too. But in his heart was a greater power, the power of God's truth, and he was not afraid.

It was early evening when Luther's turn came. The torches on the walls burned brightly. The emperor and his princes sat to hear Luther's answer. Do you admit that your writings are full of heresy and error? they asked him.

Luther answered carefully, in German. He explained what he believed from the Bible, which, said he, stands above popes and councils who have often made mistakes. He pleaded for the church to understand. Though the room grew hot and stuffy, Luther repeated patiently in excellent Latin all that he had said.

Now answer clearly whether you take back what you have written, said the emperor and his princes. Luther replied in a firm voice, "My conscience has been taken captive by the words of God. I cannot revoke anything, nor do I wish to, since to go against one's conscience is neither safe nor right. Here I stand. I can do no otherwise. So help me God. Amen."

If the friendly Prince Frederick had not ordered his soldiers to kidnap Luther and hide him, Luther would have died for his brave words. Instead he was kept in the lonely Wartburg Castle for a year before he appeared again among his people. While hiding in the castle he wrote a catechism book which the Lutheran churches still use today. He translated the Bible into beautiful German so that all the people could read the lost book for themselves. He wrote hymns for the church. Many times we have sung the fighting song, "A Mighty Fortress is our God." We love the Christmas carol, "Away in a Manger," which Luther wrote later, probably for his own children.

Many princes of Germany began to believe what Luther taught from the Bible. They led their people to follow him. And so a new kind of church, later called Lutheran after its leader, was founded in Germany. The strong Roman church fought to keep its power over the world. But the power was being broken, first in Germany and then in Switzerland and in the northern countries of Europe.

The Reformation of the church had begun. In its beginnings it said three things, speaking them from the Word of God:

The Bible is above all, said the Reformation. It is above popes and councils. It is the final word.

We are saved only by faith in Christ. We cannot add anything to his work by our works and prayers and money.

Every Christian himself can go straight to God. Because Christ has opened the way, he need not go through saints and priests.

It was Martin Luther who struck the opening blow. After him came other brave leaders, and with them a multitude of people in many lands. So began the great group of churches which we today call Protestant, because they protested against the evils in the church of Rome.

A FRENCHMAN WRITES IN HIDING

God used the son of a German miner to open the Reformation. He used the grandson of a French boatman to put it into writing and to show people how it made a difference in everything they did. Martin Luther was the one. John Calvin was the other.

The miner's son was twenty-five years old when the boatman's grandson was born. The boatman had turned to barrelmaking in a little town where the river flowed by to the sea. But his son Gerard did not care to work with staves and hoops. He was a clever young man and he followed the road over the low green hills to the bigger town of Noyon. Here he became secretary to the bishop and married the beautiful daughter of a retired innkeeper. Five boys were born in the home of Gerard Calvin. The fourth was named John.

One day, when John was twelve years old, he knelt before the bishop in the cathedral. He wore a black robe and carried a candle. The bishop cut five locks of hair from the boy's head and blessed him. With this ceremony John became a chaplain and received money from the church each year. He could not work for the church until he became a priest at twenty-five, but his head was shaved with a special haircut, the tonsure, to show that he was on his way to the priesthood.

With the yearly money from the church, father Gerard sent his son to the best university in Paris. School mornings John got up in the dark before five o'clock and shivered as he dressed in his cold room. From five in the morning until eight at night the students sat in classes with short times off to eat. After the long hours on the wooden benches, John studied in his room until midnight. With his fine mind and sure memory, he was gathering treasures of knowledge for the years ahead. He learned to speak and write excellent Latin, which was then the language of scholars as well as of the church. When he was only eighteen, John Calvin received his master of arts degree.

But at this time Calvin's father was put out of the church because of a quarrel with his bishop. So he decided to make a lawyer, not a priest, out of his son John. The young student left Paris and his priesthood studies as his father wished. In law John did as well as he had at the university in Paris. His thinking became clear and sure. Professors asked him to teach their classes when they had to be away.

But now John Calvin studied more than law. He began to study the Bible for himself, and he found a man to teach him Greek so he could read the New Testament in the language in which it was written. God sent light on those pages. He changed the heart of Calvin. He showed him from the Bible that the church on earth could be right only if it started all over again, following the example of the apostles. Meanwhile Calvin's father had died. Free now, and on his own, Calvin turned from law and the priesthood to studying the Bible full-time. I must study and write, he told himself, and looked for a quiet place where he could do this.

But quiet places were hard to find. Wherever Calvin went, people found him and begged him to teach them the truths of the Bible which the church kept from them. "Alas," he said, "all my hiding places are turned into schools."

The king was burning men for their new faith, so Calvin met the people secretly. At one place he spoke in a cave outside the city gates. But he was never safe. Twice he was put in prison. Once he escaped from his back window down a rope made of bed sheets, while friends kept his enemies at the front door. He left the town walking, disguised as a vineyard keeper with a hoe over his shoulder.

John Calvin

To find peace, Calvin finally left his own country and traveled on horseback to the Swiss city of Basel. Here, calling himself by another name to keep people from his door, he settled down to study and write. And so it happened that in the town of Basel there was published the greatest book ever written for the churches that broke away from Rome. The author was John Calvin of Noyon and he was only twenty-six years old when the book was first printed. It was called *Institutes of the Christian Religion.*

Calvin wrote the *Institutes* because he wanted to speak for the persecuted people of the Reformation in France. The French king was spreading false stories about why he killed them. They are dangerous and troublemakers, he said. Since the people could not speak for themselves, Calvin wanted to tell the world about the faith for which they were ready to die.

In the *Institutes* Calvin put a preface to the French king himself.

When I began this work, Sire, nothing was farther from my thoughts than writing a book which would afterwards be presented to your Majesty. . . . But when I saw the fury of certain men in your kingdom had grown to such a height as to leave no room for sound doctrine, I thought I should . . . exhibit my confession to you, that you may know . . . the doctrine which is the object of such unbounded rage to the madmen who are disturbing the country with fire and sword.

View our cause, most valiant king, and count us of all wicked men most wicked if you do not discover plainly that to this end we both labor and suffer reproach, because we put our hope in God, and because we believe it to be life eternal to know the only true God and Jesus Christ whom he has sent.

Calvin wrote the *Institutes* in Latin, in free-flowing, beautiful Latin. He explained with clear complete thinking what the Bible teaches. The Roman church had many books, but here was the first masterpiece of the churches of the Reformation. It has become the greatest and most lasting masterpiece, too. Today people can read it in ten languages. No one can fully tell what the *Institutes* of John Calvin have done to people and churches and countries from that day until now. The book is bigger today than it was at the first printing. Three times Calvin added to it. The last time he was so ill that he prayed for life to finish it.

A CITY REFORMED

John Calvin did more than write a great book. He put the book into practice by turning a wicked city into a city of God. This he never planned to do. He hoped to study and write in the quiet of his library. "But," he says, "God thrust me into the game."

The Swiss city of Geneva was a busy place. Through it went the highway for trade between France and Italy and the lands of the north. Merchants and travelers were always passing through Geneva, bringing new ideas from many places. It was a beautiful city, mirrored in a blue lake and shadowed by snowcapped mountains. But it was a wicked city.

Geneva was a free city, serving no king. It ruled itself by councils of its own men. When the Reformation began to spread, Geneva decided to be done with the church of Rome, for it was tired of pleasing and paying the pope. Down came the images, out went the indulgence sellers and the priests. In came new preachers, one of them a bold little man named Farel, whose voice could outshout the clanging of church bells and whose temper was as fiery as the red of his hair. But Farel found that many people were not ready to follow the Reformation. They wanted it only because they thought it would leave them free to do as they pleased. So Geneva remained a wicked city, full of taverns and drunkards, fighting and cheating, evil words and evil deeds. Farel preached on, but he was discouraged.

One summer night a young traveler stopped in a Geneva inn. He was John Calvin returning from Italy and France. On the road he had planned to take, there was a detour because it was full of soldiers getting ready for a war. So he went around to the south and took the highway through Geneva. Calvin was surprised that night by a knock on his door. He thought no one knew that he was there. But Farel had found it out and had decided that Calvin must stay to help him establish the Reformation faith in this free city of Geneva.

It was not easy to convince Calvin that Geneva was the place for him, I am shy, he pleaded, and I have no heart for public life with its fightings and dangers. I am often sick. I can serve God best from my study. But Farel would not take no for an answer. His booming voice argued and pleaded. Finally he pointed a long finger at Calvin and said, "I declare unto thee, on the part of God, that if thou refuse to labor with us here in God's work, he will curse thee, for in pleading thy studies as an excuse for abandoning us, thou seekest thyself more than God."

Calvin bowed his head. It was, he later said, "as if God had stretched forth his hand upon me from on high to arrest me." He got his few belongings from Basel and came back to Geneva, sick with a cold.

Three stormy years later Calvin and Farel left Geneva. The Council of 200 had ordered them to leave the city. Calvin had done his best to preach and to make the churches pure. But the people were not ready to hear "that Frenchman." They called him names and shook their sticks at him when he walked through the streets in his long black cloak. They sang dirty songs under his window. One night someone fired fifty shots outside his door. When Calvin would not change his mind about what he believed the church should be, the council gave him three days to get out of the city.

Another three years later the councils and the people spoke differently. Things had gone from bad to worse in the free city of Geneva. Now the councils were begging Calvin to come back to help them. But Calvin had gone to Germany and was happy in a peaceful church at Strasbourg. When a herald delivered him the letter from the councils, he was not eager to open it.

"Our good brother and particular friend," they called him now. "On the part of the Little, Great, and General Councils, we pray you very earnestly to . . . return to your former place . . . and we hope by the grace of God that this will be . . . for the fruit of the Holy Gospel, seeing that our people greatly desire you among us, and promise to behave themselves to you in a way with which you will be content."

No, Calvin told himself, I will not go back. I shudder to remember the years that I was there. To a friend he wrote, "There is no place under heaven that I am more afraid of."

Yet he did go back, and this time he went back to stay. For the twenty-three years until he died, Calvin gave his all to Geneva. He was only a minister there. He never held an office in the government. The councils did not even make him a citizen of the city until the year before he died. But they listened to him. One by one he overcame his enemies and came to rule the city. Through the mind and will which God gave this sick pale man, Geneva became the Reformation city of the world.

There was a key to Calvin's success. First he gave his whole self to God. On his seal, which has become the seal of the Christian Reformed college named in his honor, there is a hand holding out a heart to God. "My heart, promptly and sincerely, I offer to thee, O Lord," say the words beneath in Latin.

Calvin expected others to give themselves to God, too. In Geneva he was hard on the people as he was hard on himself. Even to the clothes they wore and the jokes they told, he wanted them to be God's people. What a struggle it was to change the wicked city of Geneva into such a godly city, even when the councils passed laws about these things and punished people who disobeyed.

Calvin did not only rule the people. He taught them, too. He

Car tout a coup son courroux rigoreux
S'embrasera ⁊ ne sauez le terme/
Lors sentirez de combien sont heureux
Ceux qui en luy ont confiance ferme.

Pfalme. III.

O Seigneur/que de gens a nuyre

diligens qui me troublent ⁊ grief suent:

Mon dieu/que d'ennemys. qui aux chãps se sont

mis/ ⁊ contre moy s'esleuent.

Certes plusieurs i en voy
Qui vont disant de moy:

Sa force est abolie/
Plus ne trouue en son Dieu
Salut en aucun lieu :
Mais c'est a eux folie.
  Car tu es mon tresseur
Bouclier ⁊ defenseur/
Et ma gloyre esprouuee.
C'est toy a brief parler
Lequel me fays aller
Hault la teste leuee.
  J'ay crie de ma voix
Au Seigneur maintes foys/
Luy faisant ma complaincte.
Et ne m'a repoulse:
Mais tousiours exauce
De sa montaigne saincte.
  Dont coucher m'en iray
En seurte dormiray/
Sans crainte de mesgarde.
Puis me reuelleray/
Et sans paour veilleray
Ayant Dieu pour ma garde.
  Cent mille hõmes de front/
Craindre ne me feront.
Encor qu'ilz l'entrepzinssent/
Et que pour m'estonner
Clorze ⁊ enuironner
De tous costez me vinssent.

A v

Pfalme CXXXVII.

E Stans assis aux ri ues aqua ti

ques De Babi lon Pleuriõs melan cho li

ques, No⁹ sou uenans du pays de Sion.

Et au millieu de l'ha bi ta ti on Ou de

regretz tant de pleurs espãdismes:Aux saulles

verdz noz harpes nous pendismes.

Lors ceulx qui la captifz nous emmenerent
De les sonner fort nous importunerent,
Et de syon les chansons reciter.
Las dismes nous, comment pourrions chanter
Ou seigneur dieu que nostre terr' honnoze,
En terr' estrang' ou point on ne l'adore?

Or toutesfois puisse oublier ma dextre
L'art de harper auant que l'on voy' estre
Hierusalem hors de mon souuenir.
Ma langue puiss' a mon palays tenir,
Si ie l'oubly' ⁊ si iamais ay l'oye
Tant que premier sa deliurance ioye.

Mais doncq seigneur en ta memoir' imprim
Les filz d'Edon qui sur Jerosolime
Crioyent au iour que l'on la destruisoit.
Souuienne toy qu'ng chascung d'eulx disoit.
A sac a sac qu'elle soit embrasee,
Et iusqu' au piedz des fondemens rasee.

D

taught them in sermons which were preached every day of the week. He taught them through books called commentaries which he wrote to explain the Bible, and which we still use today. He taught the children through a catechism book he wrote just for them.

Calvin began his own university in Geneva. Learned professors from many parts of Europe came to teach in it. Even Calvin's old Latin professor joined him here. Students came from many places, too. When the university was ten years old, it had sixteen hundred students. Here was the first Protestant university in the world.

Calvin taught the people something else. He taught them to sing in church again. For hundreds of years they had stood to worship without opening their mouths. Now from every Geneva church came the praise songs of the people themselves. In strong tuneful music the words of the psalms poured from their mouths and hearts. Calvin had two men in Geneva write a songbook, a larger songbook than the one he published first in Strasbourg. It was called the Genevan Psalter and we use many of its tunes today. One of the men made the psalms into poems. The other wrote tunes to fit the poems. Children practiced singing the psalms every day in school. Singing teachers practiced them with the grownups at special times.

The early church of the apostles had sung to God. A thousand years later the people of the Reformation began singing to him again. And they are still singing today.

From Calvin's book and Calvin's city comes much that you and I have seen in our churches all our lives. There are elders and deacons and ministers, not popes and bishops. The sermon is the most important part of Sunday worship. Only people who confess Christ take the bread and wine of the Lord's Supper. We have

49

seen these things and more, because we are children of God after the way of John Calvin.

But all this was new and strange in Geneva four hundred years ago. Calvin did not start with what the church of Rome had done, making some changes in it. He started from nothing, nothing but the Bible. From it alone he built all he believed about the church, and about schools and governments and every other part of life. Geneva was the first living picture of some of this. What a new picture it was.

People came from everywhere to see Geneva and to listen to Calvin. Some came to stay because the church of Rome would have burned them at home. Others came to learn and then they bravely took back to their own lands the ideas of Calvin. Those who could not come themselves talked to Calvin by letter. He never let them down. The letters streamed in and the answers poured out of Calvin's study. He wrote advice to kings and cheer to poor men in prison. Thirty-five volumes of Calvin's letters have been saved and these are not all of them.

All this Calvin did as a sick man. Fevers and headaches, arthritis, tuberculosis, and stomach troubles bothered him most of his life. When he could not work at his desk, he worked in bed, propped on pillows. When his long fingers ached too much to bend around a pen, he spoke the words to faithful secretaries. When he was too weak to walk to a place, he had himself carried there.

Nothing was too small to be important. He found houses and servants and even wives for those who needed them. The councils asked him to judge paintings and poems, to say whether a new kind of heating system was good, to decide whether the first dentist in Geneva should have a license.

At last the man of the dark brilliant eyes, of the thin pale face and the pointed chin covered by a pointed beard, the poor man who would not let the councils pay him when he was sick, the preacher and teacher and ruler of Geneva who never found the quiet study he wanted — this mighty child of God, John Calvin, left his city on earth. It was in the end of May, 1564, and he had just become fifty-five years old. The people of his earthly city walked slowly and sad-faced behind his body as it went to lie in the common grave for which he had asked.

Today no one is sure where the grave of Calvin is. But it does not matter. What matters is that the message of Calvin which changed the world four hundred years ago is still working in the world today.

GOING OUT AND GOING BACK

We could follow the spirit of John Calvin to many lands. People called that spirit Calvinism, to stand for all that Calvin believed from the Bible. Calvinism reached out to change churches and governments all over Europe. We could even follow it across the ocean to see the spirit of Calvin in the men who made the United States a nation free under God.

But before we turn to the New World, we are going to the land where sturdy people built walls to push back the sea. They worked their fields with all their strength, and they believed with all their hearts that men should be free before God. When Calvinism came to people such as these, it came to stay. In Holland, the land of sea walls and windmills, the church that followed Calvin called itself by the name he liked. The Reformed Church, it was called, because it had been formed again according to the Bible.

The church in the Netherlands sealed its faith with the blood of many martyrs. Spain was ruling Holland with an iron hand in the years after 1550 when Calvinism became strong among the Dutch. Anyone who stands against the church of Rome stands against me, said the Spanish king. He sent cruel dukes to carry out his orders. All along the streets of Holland houses became empty. The families who had eaten and slept in them were gone, burned to death, beheaded, buried alive, or drowned. Eighteen thousand died, killed for the faith they would not give up.

The Dutch people rose up and fought against the cruel rule of Spain. Eighty years they fought. As Dutchmen they fought for a free country. As Calvinists they fought for a free church, and for the Reformed faith which they declared so masterfully at the great 1618 Synod of Dort. The Spanish laughed at them and called them beggars, but in the end it was the Dutch Sea Beggars who won the victory and defeated the mighty fleet of Spain.

Holland was free at last, in 1648. Her people were free to serve God as they chose.

But the freedom was not all a blessing. The Reformed Church now became the state church of the Netherlands, and soon found itself fighting another battle. This was the endless struggle against the government's interfering in the life and business of the church. It was also a fight to keep the church pure and true even though as a state church it was the church of all the people. Besides, for many years the government would not allow the churches to hold a national gathering to settle problems and points of false doctrine that had crept into the church.

Meanwhile, all over Europe and especially in France, something new had been happening. People were beginning to think. They were so proud of this new thinking that they said they could do it without God. Some said there was no God except thinking, which they called Reason. This new god Reason made churches empty and closed their doors.

It even made its mark on the Reformed churches in the Netherlands. Now a new kind of sermon was preached. Do good to others and follow the great man Jesus, the ministers began to say. Jesus is not really God and man is not really bad and the Bible is not actually God speaking — that is what they meant to tell their people.

In 1816 the king, William I, added to the trouble. He pressed his royal seal on a law that took away the church's own government, and made the church completely a servant of the state.

Does not all this sound like a story we have heard before? Do you remember the people who died for Christ under the emperors of Rome? Do you remember Constantine, who tied the church and state together? And do you remember the centuries when the church fell far away from the Bible? God sent the

Reformation, and new churches came out of the old one to teach the truth again. Now the years have passed and one of these new churches is in the same trouble. First it was pure while it suffered under Spain. But when it was free from persecution and favored by the state, the church turned toward other voices than the voice of God.

No one listened to the men in the Netherlands who wanted to go back to the Bible. No one except the poor people, and they were without power. So God sent the Dutch Reformed Church a little reformation of its own. Out of it came a new church, preaching the whole truth of God again after the way of John Calvin.

The new church was small and poor and hated when it first came out of the old church. Five ministers led the people who left the old Reformed Church. Reverend De Cock was the leader; it was his pen that wrote the first letter of leaving in the autumn of 1834.

We do not leave the old church to make something new, he wrote. We leave it to go back to what the old church has lost. It has lost the true faith. It has left the creeds of our fathers, which it believed when it began. We secede, we go out from the old church to find this faith of our fathers again.

De Cock signed the letter and after him deacons and elders and many members of his church took the pen and added their names to the list.

The old church was angry. Stop these seceders, it asked the king. Protect the old Reformed Church, the state church, from these rude people. The king listened to the voices in the old church, of which he was the head. He ordered the seceders to hold no meetings that looked like a church service. The soldiers of the king and the guards in every town carried out the order.

But the constitution of our land gives free worship to all, pleaded the seceders in a special letter to the king. No, replied the king, this freedom is not for new churches that have been started since the constitution was made. You only disturb the peace of the land. I will not pay your ministers or build your churches. And if more than twenty of you meet together, I will have your meeting broken up and your leaders punished.

And he did. De Cock spent three months in jail. Big fines hung over the heads of the ministers. Guards and soldiers did their duty. Sometimes they marched to houses, sometimes to barns, and in warmer weather to the open fields where the seceders had met to worship. Dominie Van Raalte, the youngest of the first five ministers, wrote to his wife as he traveled from town to town, preaching: "Dear wife, I hope you do not become discouraged because of these persecutions. Dear wife, it is my calling to preach, and if it costs money, that belongs to God, and . . . he will not leave us. For a short time it will be bad here, and then we shall have to leave everything behind, and what would happen then if we did not have a treasure in heaven?"

Many people hated the seceders. They crowded around the houses where the seceders met and made noise to bother them. They threw cobblestones onto the tile roofs and sometimes broke windows and kicked in the door. When the soldiers would stop a meeting, the townspeople would move forward to get their hands on the seceders. They pushed them down and ripped their clothes and threw mud at them, shouting names and angry words. Seceders lost their jobs and no one would give them work.

After ten years the new church was still poor and hated, but it was no longer small. Through the hard years it had grown, until now it had many ministers and thousands of members. The king's orders still stood, but soldiers and people became tired of rushing to break up seceder meetings. In their hearts they still hated the new church, but their hands turned to other things.

BRAVE PEOPLE WEIGH ANCHOR

One September day a schoolteacher stopped at the home of a seceder minister. I come to say goodbye, he told the minister, because I am on my way to a ship that will take me to America. He reached into his pocket and held out two letters for the minister to read. You know the men who wrote these letters, said the schoolteacher to the minister. Read them and you will see what a fine life they have in the wonderful America. They eat meat three times a day. There the poor man is as good as the rich, and everyone is free to live as he chooses. That is the place for me.

When the schoolteacher was gone, the minister called Dominie Van Raalte to come over. Together they read the letters. What a land this must be, they said to each other. Maybe this is God's way for some of our poor troubled seceders.

Many in Holland were talking about America. Especially the poor people grew restless as they talked about this new land. Their life was a hard one. The government took big taxes from them, and when the taxes had been paid, there was almost nothing left.

Besides, the poor people were very hungry. For months they had eaten no meat. It cost too much. This they could stand as long as they had their fields of potatoes. Good wholesome potatoes the poor people ate at almost every meal. But then a terrible thing happened. Throughout the north of Europe and across the channel in England and Ireland spread a potato plague. First the leaves of the plant turned black. Then the root itself became rotten. A bad smell went up from the potato fields. Farmers saw the plague sweep through their precious crop and knew no way to stop it. Now what would the poor people eat?

The seceders were poor, too. But there was something that hurt them more than the taxes and the potato plague. Being hungry in their bodies was bad, but it was not as bad as being hungry in their souls. Two things the seceders wanted—freedom for their church, and schools where they could teach their children according to the faith they believed.

No wonder Van Raalte and his minister friend thought about America as a place where these longings might be fulfilled. Some families had already gone. Why should not a whole group of seceders go to America, buy land together in a new western state, and form a colony where the government and the churches and the schools would all be their own and truly Christian?

A society was begun to plan for this. It had a long name, Society of Christians for the Holland Emigration to the United States of America. The society began to collect money to buy land in America. It even made a constitution which said what the colony in America should be like.

Now who would go? To go to America was a bold step. Everyone had ideas about it.

Some said,

We do wrong to leave the land of our fathers. God wants us to stay here. Besides, America is not a good land. In the wild west of it there is no law. Animals and Indians kill the white people. The air is not healthy. It brings sickness to new settlers so that they pine away and die. In the busy east along the ocean, men have forgotten God and try to stir up trouble for the old lands in Europe. They are greedy to steal the money of the immigrant with false promises. Even though we suffer, it is better that we stay here. America is not for us.

But others, braver and more ready, said,

It is good to go. In America the air is free. Any man may serve God as he chooses. We will have our own mayors and churches and schools. We will have our own fields. The land is good for planting. It is cheap to buy. Miles and miles of it lie waiting to be taken, while here thirty men rush over when one farm is for sale. In America we will settle together and work together and worship together. Surely we are helping to carry out God's order that we go out to fill the earth.

Thus the fathers and mothers talked. They talked of little else. The children watched their parents' faces carefully. They whispered together about the big thing that was being decided. Would theirs be a family to go? What would it be like? Half eager, half afraid, they waited.

The list was growing. Each week more families decided to go. Van Raalte himself had not planned to go. But as the first families got themselves ready for the trip, he wondered who would lead them and preach to them in their new colony. How can I let them go alone? he asked himself as he lay recovering from typhus fever. If God strengthens me again I must go with them to be their leader, and to establish the colony for all the others who will come later.

Captain Tully Crosby waited for his passengers at the docks of Rotterdam. His ship of three masts was called the *Southerner*, and he had sailed it over from Boston. His crew had loaded on board the endless trunks and boxes of the one hundred nine Dutch people whom he was taking back to America. All but the minister's family were traveling in the hold of the ship. Each had paid his fourteen dollars for the trip, or someone had paid it for him. Every family carried enough food to feed itself during the long days at sea. There were pounds and pounds of salted meat, rice, flour, potatoes, and dried peas, a little butter and cheese, some coffee and some tea.

Strong deckhands pulled up the anchors. The *Southerner* moved slowly on its way toward the open sea. September 24, 1846, wrote Captain Crosby in his ship's log. He thought a moment about those passengers who had been kneeling on the dock to pray. What a song they had sung, one of their church songs, more than likely.

A cold wind caught the sails and filled them. For a time the people on deck could see the dear shores of Holland. Then they could see only a low grey shape sinking into the sea. They strained their eyes, still looking. But there was only water now. Slowly they turned away from the land they had left and prayed that the new land to which they were going would be right for them.

A MAN AND HIS DREAM

Today a good ship crosses the Atlantic Ocean in five days. Captain Crosby needed fifty-five days for the winds to bring his *Southerner* into the noisy port of New York. Some days the wind whispered and the sails hung limp. Other days the wind whipped the waves into giant green mountains and sent the sailing ship crashing from the top to the bottom of each. On such days the passengers huddled together in the stale crowded hold, wondering whether they would ever again stand safely on dry land.

Not everyone who went up the gangplank in Rotterdam was there when the boat docked. Two little children and a man had died from illness. Wrapped in white sheets with weights of sand, their bodies had been sadly let down into the deep waters of the ocean.

It was a Wednesday in November when Van Raalte and his people first stood on the ground of their new land. How tired they were of the swaying ship, the salty meat, and the hard bread. Can we have a drink of water now? begged the children. Where are we going next?

In this strange busy place there was someone to meet them. What a surprise. The man spoke good Dutch, too. Look, said Van Raalte to his people after he had talked with the man, this is Dominie De Witt of a Dutch Reformed church here in New York City. He saw a letter I wrote to America last year, and he is here to help us. See how well God takes care of us.

Signs of snow were in the sky and the tree branches were bare. We must hurry on to our new home before the winter stops us, Van Raalte told Dominie De Witt.

First there was a steamboat chugging up the Hudson River to Albany. The weary people, some in wooden shoes, boarded it with all their trunks and boxes. In Albany another kind minister, Dominie Wyckoff, was ready to help. You can best take the train from here to Buffalo, he said. I will get the tickets for you. When others come to join you, my church and I will help them, too.

At Buffalo there was a second steamer to take. It was waiting in the harbor because the lake called Erie was rough and angry. Finally the steamer blew its whistle and started on the last trip it would make before winter. It docked in Detroit, the biggest busiest city in the new state of Michigan.

62

Van Raalte had hoped to take another boat around the Michigan peninsula to the west side of the state. Across the lake from Michigan on that side is Wisconsin. While he was still in the Netherlands, Van Raalte had thought much of Wisconsin. The name Milwaukee, Wisconsin, was on his trunks. But in America people spoke of Michigan as a better place for the new colony.

No more boats until spring, said the shipping captains in Detroit. There was ice forming on the lakes at the top of the peninsula and it was dangerous to go through. To cross Michigan over land would have cost too much for a group of people with all their baggage. So the people stayed where they were. Some worked for a kind shipbuilder. Van Raalte went on alone, to scout out a place for the colony. Perhaps I will go also to Wisconsin and Chicago and down the Mississippi River to St. Louis, he told his wife. But first I will look in Michigan.

A slow snorting train went out of Detroit and part way across the state. Van Raalte took it as far as Kalamazoo. Then he hired a sleigh to go to Allegan, because it was December and the ground was white with snow. In his mind he knew what kind of place he must find. It should have trees for homes and heat and furniture. It should have rivers or streams for traveling and for fish. The land should be good for farming after the trees were cut down. It should be a new, unsettled place where the colony could grow and spread out. And perhaps a place could be found in Michigan where a river emptied into the big lake, so that the colony could send and receive people and goods by water all the way to the busy east of America.

At Detroit the men of the state government told Van Raalte there was land like that for sale in the western part of Michigan. They liked this slim bearded man, and they saw in him a good leader in spite of the broken English he spoke. The men of the government gave Van Raalte names of men to see. Go see Judge Kellogg in Allegan, they said, and Reverend George Smith, the

63

white missionary to the Ottawa Indians, and Isaac Fairbanks, whom the government has sent to teach the Indians how to farm.

With the judge and the minister and Mr. Fairbanks, all three of them eager to help, Van Raalte explored the streams and forests. Day after day they tramped through deep snow, following Indian trails or pushing through thickets. They crossed icy brooks, dug through snow to see what kind of soil was there, and noticed the trees and animals around them. Judge Kellogg gave Van Raalte extra clothes and snowshoes, but Van Raalte was not used to the long hikes. Sometimes he sank down in the snow to rest, saying in his poor English, "I can no more, I can no more." Then he thought of the people depending on him, waiting for him to find a spot for the new colony. So he went on, praying for strength, and for wisdom to choose the right place.

Two rivers flowed into the big lake in the area Van Raalte explored. The Grand and the Kalamazoo rivers were thirty miles apart, and each of them already had a little city where the river met the lake. There was Grand Haven at the mouth of the Grand and Saugatuck at the mouth of the Kalamazoo. Halfway between these rivers was a smaller stream called the Black River. It emptied into a long narrow lake, and the tip of this lake touched the big lake, with only a few sandbars between. Here were the Ottawa Indians, living in wigwams with their chief, Chief Peter Wakazoo, in a settlement called Old Wing Mission.

In this place, Van Raalte told himself after weeks of looking, I can picture the colony. The dream became clearer in his mind. I can see houses and churches and schools and roads, boats on the narrow lake and a channel to the big lake that will connect us with the outside world, sawmills and factories, farms where the trees have been cut down. It will not be done in a year, or in five years. It will be hard work. But it will come. God helping us, it will surely come.

God gives dreams to great men so that others can follow these leaders and work to make the dreams come true. This was such a man with his dream. He stood alone in two feet of snow with only wild forests and swampland around him. Here the little river met the long narrow lake and the bears and wolves came out of the woods to drink. But Van Raalte's dream looked far beyond the lonely land and the tangled trees which no white man had tamed. He saw whole cities of Dutch Christians spreading out in western Michigan. He saw them serving God after the way of John Calvin and the early church, and he hoped they would be strong enough to let their light shine clearly in the new land of America.

THE DREAM BEGINS TO COME TRUE

The rain and snow dripped through the roof of the first log cabin. Six men came on ahead to build it. They had never chopped trees before, and at first they hacked round and round the trunk and then ran for cover when the tree began to fall. The Indians and Mr. Fairbanks taught the men the right way to cut down trees. Many of the trees were so big that three men could not touch hands around one of them. There was no way to make boards and shingles, so the roof as well as the sides of the rough cabin was made of split logs, with moss pressed into the cracks between. Even in winter with all the leaves gone, the little cabin looked quite swallowed up in the big forest.

Several families arrived by sleigh to live in the first log cabin. They had no beds or tables, and no stoves for cooking. The Indian squaws showed the white women how to bake bread by laying balls of dough in hot ashes, and how to soften ears of corn in iron kettles of water and wood ashes hung over the open fire. For the first few months it seemed as if there was only corn for every meal, with coffee made from roasted corn to drink. Meanwhile the men were working on the second cabin, so that more families could squeeze into it together until there were cabins for everyone.

Van Raalte wrote letters to tell where the new colony was. He wrote to the seceders in the Netherlands, and to the kind Reverend Wyckoff in Albany. He wrote the people who were left in

Detroit and some who were waiting in other towns. I have bought thousands of acres, he wrote, some from the Indians, some from a Mr. Palmer of New York, and the rest from the government of Michigan and the federal government of the United States. We have named our colony Holland. Come join us in this wonderful new place God has given us.

With bright hopes, families packed their belongings and made the long ocean trip. We are going to Van Raalte, they said, and in their minds they pictured the new Holland as a lovely growing town.

When spring came, steamers could take new settlers around the peninsula to the harbor at Grand Haven. Here the new people transferred all their trunks and boxes to a flatboat pulled by horses walking along the beach. The horses pulled them eighteen miles farther along the shore of the big lake and then let them off in the soft light-colored sand.

But where is Holland? asked the people, looking around in dismay. The owner of the flatboat waved his hand toward the dune, and turned his horses back toward Grand Haven.

In the shelter of the dune there was a shack of driftwood and logs. Van Raalte had the men make it for the new people to use until their things could be brought to the far end of the narrow lake, where the beginnings of new Holland were. Here were the log cabins, connected by muddy paths and almost hidden among the tall trees. And here again the newcomers looked around in dismay, asking, This—is this new Holland?

The people came faster than cabins could be built for them. So the men piled hemlock branches against tree trunks and stretched sheets or blankets over them to make huts. But the rain trickled into the hemlock huts. Sometimes a big black snake came in, too, quite uninvited.

68

The spring rains filled the swamplands, and the dampness of the swamps and of the huts and cabins brought a fever to the people. In every family there was sickness, with no doctor and little medicine to help.

Many people died. Fathers and mothers had to bury their own children. Boys and girls cried for their dead parents, and other kind families took them in. Because people needed homes so badly, the men who were well could not stop building cabins to make enough coffins for burying. Some bodies were carefully wrapped in sheets and buried beneath big trees. The wild grasses and flowers grew over them and soon no one could tell which tree had a grave beneath its shady branches.

It was a sad time. The tired people worked on, but their hearts were heavy. Had they come to the new land to die? Even Van Raalte, the man with the dream, cried out as he prayed one Sunday morning, "O Lord, must we all die?" Around him sat the people who were left. They sat on fallen trees and stumps in their outdoor church. Their heads were bowed. Even their shoulders were bowed because they were so discouraged.

It was very quiet after Van Raalte cried out to God. Only the birds and squirrels made their little noises. After the quiet Van Raalte finished his prayer. After the prayer he preached.

It was a good sermon, as all his sermons were. After that Sunday God took the sickness away. He put new hope into the hearts of Van Raalte and his people. He began to make the dream come true.

Even in the dark days, there were the joys of weddings and of babies born and baptized. Life was going ahead, not stopping, in the new colony. It went ahead in faith, a deep faith that God would bless the hard beginnings and turn them into prosperous lands and villages.

Only two years after the first log cabin was built, there were eight different villages of Dutch people in western Michigan. There were Holland and Zeeland and Vriesland and Graafschap

and Overisel and North Holland and Noordeloos and Drenthe, all like little pieces of the Netherlands after which they were named. New Holland itself had streets and more than two hundred houses. Soon there were stores and hotels and factories, a newspaper, and roads over which the stagecoach came with regular mail. Men standing waistdeep in water shoveled away the sandbars to make a channel so that flatboats could pass from the big lake into the long narrow one and so on to the city of Holland.

Of course there was a church in every settlement, and in Holland, the beginning of a Christian college. Log cabins and log churches were disappearing, and in their places came new sturdy buildings, some of them still used today. This was Van Raalte's colony of Dutch people, reaching out to fill western Michigan with its farms and towns.

THE JOINING

We have come almost to the beginning of our own Christian Reformed Church in America. It is not such a happy beginning, even though it had to come. The happy part about it is what God has done with the poor beginning.

Remember we talked about the kind Dutch ministers in New York and Albany who helped Van Raalte on his way to Michigan? They helped thousands of other Dutch settlers, too, and made a friendly gateway to America for these tired people in a strange land. The ministers met the boats, protected the people from swindlers, fed the people and housed them, found them work and gave them money, cared for their sick and buried those who died on the way. For people who spoke a strange language and had never before traveled more than a few miles from their Dutch farms and windmills, this help was a wonderful thing.

Where did these kind ministers come from? How did they happen to be already in America?

Two hundred years before Van Raalte came to America, Dutch sea captains were looking for a new way to sail their trading ships to India. Instead of going around the bottom of South America, they hoped to find a quicker and less stormy way somewhere in the north. In 1611 an English captain, Henry Hudson, sailed a Dutch ship named the *Half Moon* to hunt for this new way. He discovered the wide river now named the Hudson River after him, and though he found it was not a channel to India, he told the Dutch merchants so much about it that some of them decided to see for themselves. They came and planted the Dutch flag on the new land to claim it for the Netherlands. More Dutch people came and settled up and down the shores of the Hudson River. The great city of New York was first a Dutch settlement called New Amsterdam.

These first Dutch people came because America was rich in land and furs and they wanted to share these riches. Of course they brought their religion along with them, the religion of the old Reformed Church in the Netherlands, and these were the days before that church drifted away from the full truth of God. But trade, not persecution, was their big reason for coming to America, a situation different from that of Van Raalte and the others who came two hundred years later.

As the years passed, the early Dutch melted into the life of America, and some changes came into their churches. Meanwhile there was war in Europe and few Dutch people crossed the ocean again until the time of Van Raalte. When this new stream of Dutch settlers came to America, they were helped by the great-great-grandchildren of the early Dutch who followed Henry Hudson. The Reverends Wyckoff and De Witt and their congregations were some of these.

Two years after the first tree was felled near Black River, the Reverend Wyckoff made a trip from Albany to visit the colony. Everyone turned out to welcome a good friend. He rode from village to village on the only horse in the colony, the elders and ministers walking beside him over the winding trails through the woods. He ate the best salt pork and potatoes and bread and coffee the settlers had, though it was quite different food than he ate at home in the east. In a letter he wrote that he had never seen such faith and praying and godly living; it was like the early days of the apostles, so beautiful it was.

Before the Reverend Wyckoff left the colony, he had a meeting with the four ministers and twenty elders and deacons to ask them an important question. Would the new churches of western Michigan, who had only each other to lean on, like to join the churches in America called the Dutch Reformed, the churches begun by the early Dutch in the east? I am sent by these churches, said Wyckoff, to ask you brethren what you think.

The men of western Michigan were not sure. They were glad the churches of the east held the same creeds. They were thankful for all the good these churches had done for them, while the seceders in the Netherlands seemed to have forgotten all about the new settlers. The men of western Michigan knew well how poor they were and how badly they needed help. But they also remembered why they had come to America, and the trouble under the old Reformed Church in the Netherlands. They did not want to get tangled up again with a church that believed differently.

Wyckoff saw what worried them, and he told them that if ever

in the future they wanted to leave the Dutch Reformed churches in America, they could do this. Van Raalte and his men promised to give their answer soon.

In the spring of 1850 Van Raalte traveled east to Albany where men from the Dutch Reformed churches were meeting. He wanted very much to join these churches. They had helped him more than anyone in the colony knew. They had even loaned him money when he needed it to buy more land, eight thousand dollars worth of land. It would seem very ungrateful to refuse to join them. And since the eastern churches believed the same creeds, surely the joining was a good thing, Van Raalte believed.

Our churches in western Michigan will become a part of you, Van Raalte told the men meeting in Albany. It was agreed that the nine new churches would be a classis by themselves, called the Classis of Holland, as they had already called themselves.

THE WEAVER

It is a good thing, said many of the people in the colony when they heard what was done. We need friends to help us, and these Dutch Reformed churches believe as we do.

But some of the people wondered about the thing that had been done. We came far and suffered much to worship God freely here, they said. This joining—did we do it too quickly? Can we be sure it is right?

At first they did not talk about it much. Maybe a man turned over such thoughts in his mind as he walked at sunset between the stumps where his corn and wheat were growing. Or a mother wondered as she kneaded her bread on the wooden table in the kitchen. As the months went by, the thoughts grew and did not go away.

There was one new Dutchman in the colony who helped the most to turn the thoughts into words and the words into action. He was a weaver, not a minister, a slim wiry man whose hair had turned white early, and whose chin was shaved, not bearded as most men's were. The eyes of the weaver were blue, bright blue, clear and piercing. When he set his lips together, they lay in a tight line with wrinkles creasing his cheeks. In the old country the weaver had often led meetings of the seceders. He was a fighter, this small man, and when he saw what he believed to be right, he would not stop until he saw it done.

Gysbert Haan was the weaver's name. The summer after Van Raalte had come, Haan made the uncomfortable ocean trip to the New World with his family of nine children. But he did not go at once to the colony. Instead he stayed two years in the east,

in the Hudson River cities of Albany and Troy. Here he saw
more of the Dutch Reformed churches in the east than did the
settlers who only passed through. Some of the things he saw in
those churches did not please him.

The ministers did not preach each Sunday from the creed called
the Heidelberg Catechism. Sometimes they baptized babies at

home instead of in the church services. The songs of these churches were more frequently hymns than the psalms which came from God's Word. Some of the members belonged to secret societies called lodges, which talked about God but did not believe in Christ as his son, our only Savior. Not all these churches were careful to teach their children in weekly catechism classes. People who were not members of the churches took the Lord's Supper with them. Slowly, the churches of the east seemed to be slipping away from the full godly believing and living which the seceders had come to America to keep.

This is no church for us to join, said the weaver. They are losing the fire from their hearts, and we cannot agree with the things they do. But shortly after the weaver came to the colony, Van Raalte's Classis of Holland did join the Dutch Reformed churches. Now what was to be done?

After his work was over for the day, Haan went knocking on the doors of the homes in the colony. He found the people who wondered in their hearts about the joining, and he told them what he had seen in the east. He stirred them up to wonder aloud to each other. From the colony he went to Grand Rapids, the city beside the rapids of the Grand River. There were factories and stores and many industries in Grand Rapids. There were churches, too, also Dutch Reformed churches belonging to the Classis of Holland. In the Second Reformed Church Haan served as elder, and he often talked with his minister and others about what he believed.

As the months went by, more and more wonderings turned into words, strong words. Some of the words were unkind words against Van Raalte. There were people who said he was trying to be the lord and master of the colony. Sometimes the two things got mixed up together, the grumbling about Van Raalte and the arguing about the joining. Van Raalte sold us to the churches of the east, said these unkind voices, forgetting how

Van Raalte had suffered and worked for his people, even though he also told them what to do.

Brothers argued together and then became too angry to speak to each other. Men gathered to talk far into the night, raising their voices and shaking their fingers. In many a house the man found it hard to pray when he went to bed, because there was more anger than love in his heart. And when he lay awake, staring into the darkness, he heard the words of the other men and spoke his own words to himself, all over again.

In the middle of the arguing, a new minister named Van den Bosch came to the colony. He did not believe in the joining either, and he, like Haan, was ready to do something about it.

Remember, said the minister to the people who agreed with him, that the Reverend Wyckoff said we were free to leave the Dutch Reformed churches at any time. If we leave them, we are only doing what he said we could do. Others have left them before. Thirty years ago some churches in the east left them to be a group by themselves. They too did not believe in what the Dutch Reformed churches were doing.

I am ready to act, said the minister Van den Bosch of Noordeloos. In Grand Rapids the weaver Haan was ready, too. And they were not the only ones.

NO LONGER TO BELONG

The church of Zeeland was the prettiest of the first churches in the colony. It was made of squared cedar logs and it had a little tower on top with a bell in it. The bell rang twice each Sunday to greet the people coming to the church from all around. It rang slowly when someone died, and on the day the funeral procession left the church, it sadly tolled the number of years of the man's life.

Perhaps the bell in the pretty Zeeland church also rang for meetings. If it did, it pealed for the all-day meeting of Classis Holland held there on April 8, 1857. Men from churches more than a few miles away had arrived for the meeting the evening before in carriages or wagons pulled by horses who picked their way carefully over the muddy roads. This was the meeting, the important meeting of the twenty men in Sunday black suits. It was the meeting when the four papers that mark the beginning of our story were read.

At the clerk's table in the front of the church when the meeting began sat Albertus Christiaan Van Raalte. His keen eyes took in the other men and he bent his bearded face to write their names with his quill pen. There were some names missing, he knew, the names of men who could have come. The minister Van den Bosch of Noordeloos was not there. Nor the minister Kleyn of Grand Rapids. Nor any elders at all from the churches of Polkton and Graafschap which had no ministers. Why?

In the pile of papers on the clerk's desk lay the answer. When it was time, Van Raalte stood to read from the four letters that told the reason.

First came one from Dominie Van den Bosch. "By this. . . I declare myself no longer to belong to you," he said. Using strong language he ended his letter this way: "I hope that your eyes may yet be opened to see your extreme wickedness, to take it to heart, and to be converted therefrom."

There was no sound in the Zeeland church but the sputtering of a stubborn little piece of wood in the iron stove. Van Raalte laid down the first letter and began the second. It came from Dominie Kleyn in Grand Rapids, who wrote with kind words about his leaving, asking that no bitterness be among the churches and wishing they could all join together to be a free church by themselves again.

Next was a longer letter from one hundred thirteen people of the hill church in Graafschap. These were the band of people who came together in the first summer of the colony and chose a broad hill four miles from Holland for their new village. The soil of the place, which they named Graafschap, was good clay soil, and the men paid a dollar and a quarter an acre for it. When Graafschap had a minister, he lived in a lean-to room attached to the side of the church, and if he needed more room to be comfortable, he moved some of his furniture onto the church platform during the week.

In Graafschap, too, the people had wondered and argued about the joining. Now they sent a letter to the classis. The letter gave reasons for leaving the Dutch Reformed churches, and then said, "Brethren, we are glad that almost the entire congregation . . . with us, the consistory, and our dear little children, again stand upon the same standpoint on which our fathers enjoyed so much blessedness, and oh, we would rejoice still more if the King of the Church should bring you to this conviction. The God of love be your . . . guide to walk in the way of truth."

The last of the four letters came next. Van Raalte read it in his quick, clear voice. It came from the church of Polkton, a younger church than the others, only three years old. The people of this church lived in the Grand River valley, and their village was called Polkton after the name of their township, not a Dutch but an American name. Today we know this place as Coopersville. Though they had no minister, the people of Polkton spoke, too. "No longer to belong," they said. At the end of their letter they used the words of the ocean that had pounded against the dikes of the old country and tossed them about on their long voyage to America. "In the hope that God, who alone is able to make a roaring sea calm and smooth, may also make your hearts so calm and smooth, that you will walk with us in the way of our fathers, is our heartfelt . . . prayer."

This is what the four letters said, those letters on the clerk's table in the bell church of Zeeland. What the letters did was to separate a group of people from the Dutch Reformed Classis of Holland. By their own writing and doing, these people now stood alone.

A SHARE IN A TREASURE

Another classis held a meeting in April, 1857. It was not the Classis of Holland, but a small new classis, a few men sitting together in the Graafschap hill church, the church with the lean-to. This was the only church where the men could sit, because it was the only church building that was theirs.

We do not know much about this little meeting. Dominie Van den Bosch was the secretary, but whatever minutes he wrote have been lost. Dominie Kleyn was president for the day, although he later went back to Classis Holland. Some elders were there, too. For one, there was elder Gelock from Grand Rapids who wrote down something about the meeting. We decided, he said, to hold a day of prayer and fasting to confess our sins before the Lord and to pray for the new church "led out."

The men met to form a classis. They did not give the classis a name, and they did not find a name for their new church either. They spoke together about what they believed and they decided to write one letter. It was a letter to the mother church, the church of the seceders in the Netherlands. The ministers Kleyn and Van den Bosch wrote the letter in Grand Rapids on April 29 and signed their names to it.

We have left the Dutch Reformed churches in America, said the letter, just as the seceders left the old Reformed Church twenty years ago in the Netherlands, to be pure and to go back to the faith of our fathers. We have prayed God to bless us and we want you to know what we have done. Count us again a part of you, as indeed we truly are.

The day of the little classis meeting was the birthday of the Christian Reformed Church. But no one is certain what day this really was, and so we often use the date of the Classis Holland

85

meeting, the day when the four letters were read. Whatever the day, the month was April and the year 1857 when the Christian Reformed Church in America had its beginning.

The beginning had not come quickly. First was the thinking and then the talking and these took six years. Then came the doing, slowly. A year before the birthday, elders Haan and Gelock resigned from their Grand Rapids church, and elder Krabshuis resigned from the church in Holland. The dignified elder Dam was put out of the Vriesland church because he spoke against the joining of 1850.

In January of the birthday year, Dominie Kleyn of Grand Rapids decided to leave Classis Holland. On the Sunday he chose to tell his people about this, he was blocked from his pulpit. Somehow the news had leaked out, and an elder stood at the steps to the platform to keep the dominie from his regular place. The congregation watched, tense and excited. From where he stood below the pulpit, Kleyn turned to the people, stretched out his arms, and cried, "Lord, I have sinned, but what wrong have these sheep done?" Then he turned and walked from the church.

For a moment no one stirred. Then the silence was broken by people moving, rising from their benches to follow their dominie out through the doorway. Half of the congregation left, and half stayed in their pews. But those who left did not go without their church service. They met in the afternoon, crowded into Gysbert Haan's parlor, where they made the timbers of his house ring with the sound of their psalms. These were the people who organized themselves into a separate church on March 19 of the birthday year.

Then came April 7, with the letters that made the leaving official. The people for whom the letters spoke were by themselves again. They were by themselves and very much alone. How poor they were in all things that could be seen and counted.

It was a very small group to think that it could stand alone. Dominie Van den Bosch brought only nineteen people with him from Noordeloos. With the one hundred thirteen from Graafschap, a few from the weak little Polkton church which soon died out altogether, and the people of Grand Rapids who numbered themselves as fifty-four families, there was only a handful, perhaps two hundred fifty adults.

The new group had no money. Its people were poor, struggling to get a start in the land to which they had come with nothing. By leaving Classis Holland, they cut themselves loose from the rich church relatives in the east who had money to give and gave it freely. They had no church buildings except the church in

Graafschap, which was theirs because more than a hundred people of that church wanted to leave Classis Holland, and only
eleven wanted to stay with it. Where would the "led out" people
worship? How would they build new churches?

The people who left in 1857 also found themselves without
friends. The harsh words on both sides had cut them apart from
the people of Classis Holland. It took many years for that wound
to heal, and the scar of it still seems to be there. Seceder minister
Scholte was in Iowa with another colony of Dutch, but he had
only sharp words when he heard about the break in Michigan.
Worst of all, the mother church in the Netherlands, to whom the
letter of the little April classis had been sent, treated the new
group like an ugly duckling, unworthy to be received. This hurt
most.

And who was to preach to the people "led out"? They had only
one minister, a man of strong convictions and strong words, but
a man who lacked a full education. There was no school to train
new ministers, no money to build one, and no man fit to teach
even if there were a school.

The new group had no name either, and it did not get one
until two years had passed.

What did the people of 1857 have? Did they have anything?

Yes, with all their being poor and weak, they had a treasure.
Sometimes they did not see the treasure clearly. They forgot
about it in the noise of their quarrelings and the pinch of their
poverty and the loneliness they felt in a strange land without
friends.

At such times God would lift up their eyes and show them that
they were not alone. Then the people of 1857 understood that
they were not a tiny forsaken beginning. In some ways they were

not a beginning at all, because a beginning means a new thing, and the break of 1857 was no new thing. It was an old thing, often done, reaching back many years to many places. Thus, 1857 was not a beginning so much as it was a returning. It was a going back to stand more squarely in the line of Christ's true church on earth. This was no new thing. Luther was returning, and Calvin too, when they left the church of Rome. In every country of Europe there was some return. In the Netherlands also, a glad return and then, years later, another return when the church of the seceders came out of the old church which was falling away.

In that great line stood the tiny return of 1857. It had nothing in itself to be proud about, and it had many sins to confess. But this was its treasure, that it meant to be a church according to the whole word of God, holding fast to the faith once for all delivered to the saints.

Weak and stumbling, the return of 1857 could look back and see some of these saints — leaders like the black-cloaked ruler of Geneva and the German monk who could "do no otherwise," the famous African son of a praying mother and the inspired missionary-writer whose thorn the Lord would not take away. Around them, coming out of many lands and many centuries, pressed the multitudes who had lived on earth to hold fast, and who had died to enter the perfect church of heaven.

Not all earthly churches stand squarely in that line, bought with Christ's blood and sealed with the blood of many martyrs. Some churches do not stand in the line at all. With all their failings, the people of 1857 were struggling to take their place more surely in it again.

As a small part of that mighty line, they knew they had a place to fill, a church to build, and a message to preach in the new land which was the melting pot of nations.

DOMINIE ALONE

The first minister of the Christian Reformed Church was an interesting man. Koene was his first name, and he was the oldest of nine children in a family called Van den Bosch. The early years of his life he lived in the Netherlands. His parents were poor and when they joined the seceders, they became still poorer. Koene began working full time to help support the family when he was only twelve.

He said about himself, "Up to twenty years I knew neither God nor myself." Then God moved him and changed him, so that he could say gladly, "When I was twenty-one, the Lord brought me from death to life." Koene Van den Bosch decided to become a seceder minister. The seceders had no seminary, so he studied with two or three ministers in the province of Drenthe where he lived. He studied hard to enlarge his small education, and his books went along with him to the heath where he read while tending sheep to earn a living.

Meanwhile some of Koene's brothers wanted to go to America to join Dominie Van Raalte. Father Van den Bosch was ready to go, but mother could not bear to leave her oldest son. Many nights she prayed the Lord to make her free to go and finally one morning she told her family she was ready. The Van den Bosch family arrived in New York harbor in June of 1848.

Meanwhile Koene went on studying in the Netherlands and he married. He and his wife did not have enough money to live, so the young Mrs. Van den Bosch took in sewing and her husband began to knit stockings which he sold. Probably he became a good knitter. If his socks were half as strong as his words often were, they were strong enough!

90

When he became minister in his first church at Elburg, Koene Van den Bosch was still poor. One Saturday night there was no food in the house, and the young minister asked the Lord what to do about his hungry family. Before bedtime a man knocked on the door, bringing a basket of bread to his dominie.

In 1853 the minister Van den Bosch was called to the church at Noordeloos, in the Dutch province of South Holland. From here he went to America in 1856 when he was thirty-eight years old, taking with him his family and twenty-nine members of his church. He was called to America by a group of people who had settled five miles from new Holland, and he preached his first sermon to them in the woods, standing in a farmer's rough wagon.

The people named their settlement Noordeloos after the place from which their new dominie had come. There were deer aplenty in the woods around Noordeloos and the settlers had their fill of venison. One man said he shot over seventy of them. Soon there was a sawmill in the settlement, too.

Dominie Van den Bosch was happy to be near his parents and his brothers again. They had settled in Zeeland, the place first called "Brothertown." He found among his Noordeloos church people someone we have met before—the schoolteacher who stopped to see a seceder minister before he left for America. This school-teacher, whose name was Hartgerink, fought with the United States army in the Mexican War and afterwards the government offered him a piece of land to reward him for his service. Hart-gerink picked and settled a plot in the area later called Noordeloos.

It was May, 1856, when Dominie Van den Bosch came to Noordeloos. Soon he was taking sides in the argument about joining the Dutch Reformed churches. He spoke strongly, some-times harshly, against the joining of 1850, and ten months after he

preached from the farmer's cart, he took action by writing the letter which was read in the bell church of Zeeland on April 8, 1857.

A few months after the birthday of the new church, Dominie Kleyn changed his mind and went back to Classis Holland. Then for six struggling years, Dominie Van den Bosch was the only minister among the people of 1857. He was tall and strong, "rough and ready," and he made his way through the woods from church to church driving a team of oxen which pulled the wagon in which he rode. In the wagon he carried a shovel to dig himself out of holes and an axe to chop down trees that blocked the trail. For his work the first minister was supposed to receive four hundred dollars a year, but often his people were unable to pay him regularly.

SMALL BEGINNINGS

There were other early leaders besides the dominie. They were elders like fiery Gysbert Haan and keen Johannes Gezon, both from Grand Rapids. Elder Gezon wrote well the minutes of the early classis meetings and was our first clerk of classis. He had lived in The Hague and served in the Dutch army as a non-commissioned officer. Under bushy eyebrows his eyes were friendly, and though he had no beard, his sideburns came down to the bottom of his ears. Elder Van Anrooy from the Graafschap church was a man of courage and action like Peter, and his companion from the hill church, elder Strabbing, reminded people more of the love and steadiness of the apostle John.

There were elders from the church in Vriesland, too, a church that joined the people of 1857 nine days after the letters were read in Zeeland. Vriesland was nine miles from Holland, and it was settled by a group of people who called a minister and formed themselves into a congregation before they left the Netherlands. Like the people of Graafschap, they wanted clay soil for farming, and they found it in the place they named Vriesland, after the Dutch province from which they came.

But the new Vriesland was deep in the forest and the trail to Holland went through marsh and brush and deep brooks without bridges. In the early years the people almost starved because provisions were so hard to get.

After huts of branches covered with cloth, the Vrieslanders first built cabins of logs stuck in the ground on end. Across these were laid other logs for a roof, and then the cracks were filled with clay. One man called his simple house The Citadel because it was covered with so much clay that he said nothing could destroy it.

The Vrieslanders held church services outdoors for the first summer. But in the fall the rains drove them inside the house of their modest dominie, who did regular work six days a week to take care of his family. Next the people met in the bigger log house of another man, where the dominie performed the first marriage, standing behind an upside down barrel for a pulpit. When this house became too small, the people built a church. As soon as its walls were up, before the roof and floor and doors, they rolled logs into it and cut them to make crude benches. Here there was room for all—also for all the mosquitoes, who sometimes bothered the dominie so much that he had to stop preaching to brush them off.

Some of these Vriesland people joined the group of 1857. The first classis meeting of which we have a record was the meeting of ten men in Vriesland on October 7, 1857.

There were more classis meetings, one each spring and one each fall. But there were still only four churches. Vriesland had come in but Polkton had gone out, so the number was the same. Four churches and one minister. With the mother church frowning on the ugly duckling, ministers from the Netherlands were not eager to come to the new church.

Often the elders and their dominie were discouraged. Once they talked about joining another kind of church instead of staying by themselves. Then elder Groen of Vriesland stood up and spoke with such stirring words that the leaders of 1857 decided to go on again.

They finally gave the new church a name in 1859. Holland Reformed Church they called it. This was soon changed to True Holland Reformed Church. Twenty years later, when the mother church recognized its true daughter in America, the name became Holland Christian Reformed Church. These three names were all in the Dutch language. Not until after 1890 did our

94

church name become simply the Christian Reformed Church, as we know it today.

This was the beginning of 1857, a poor and a weak beginning. There was nothing in it to make us proud of ourselves, and everything in it to make us thrilled with what God has brought out of the poor beginning.

I will have my glory, God seems to say, also through the church in America called Christian Reformed. It is I who will build it and teach it and use it.

O powerful gracious God, by thy spirit humble us and use us also today.

A SCHOOL IN PARSONAGE AND UPPER ROOM

We must have ministers, trained ministers, if we are to live and grow. We cannot count on getting them from the Netherlands, so we must train them here. At least we must make a beginning.

This was the minister Van den Bosch, the only minister, speaking to the classis in the Spring Street church of Grand Rapids. It was 1861, in the cold of February.

The seven voting elders heard him and they nodded while the clerk, elder Krabshuis, wrote it down. But the nodding and the writing did not get it done.

Two years later the minister Van den Bosch was speaking again to the classis. Now he was no longer the only minister. To the church of Grand Rapids had come Dominie Van Leeuwen from the Netherlands. Van Leeuwen had also been a schoolteacher in the old land, and he wrote well.

I speak again about a matter dear to my heart, said Dominie Van den Bosch to the men who were sitting this time in Zeeland. We must begin to train our own ministers. The churches from which we come have always had educated ministers. We must be worthy to stand in their line. Dominie Van Leeuwen has more schooling than I have had. I propose that he begin to teach in his parsonage any who wish to be ministers in our churches.

Ja, said the men of classis, and the thing was done. No, not done, only begun. Nine months later the first student said his first lesson in "the school in the parsonage." But the teacher of the school moved to a church in New Jersey which had called him. So the school moved, too, and the teaching went on, now in the parsonage of Graafschap.

In this parsonage was the third minister of the Christian Reformed Church, a remarkable man. Dominie Douwe Johannes Vander Werp, a well-trained minister who had served five churches in the Netherlands, came to the people of 1857 and gave them the last eleven years of his busy life. He preached, he taught, he traveled, and he wrote. He was a steady loyal man, wise and gifted.

Dominie Vander Werp helped to organize new churches and he was a faithful minister in his own church. He was also the first editor of our first church paper, *De Wachter*. Everyone of 1857 read *De Wachter*. They read no English papers or magazines and so they depended on *De Wachter—The Watchman—*to tell them everything. Through the wise progressive ideas of the first editor they learned much.

Besides all this, the third dominie prepared students to be ministers. Two mornings every week they came to the parsonage, turning off the dirt road at the little white-fenced yard. Through the gate, past the big shade tree, and along the worn path to the back door they went. The neighbor women would watch from behind their window curtains to see the students go in. There were four of them when the Graafschap dominie first began to teach.

Each student preached his first sermon in the Graafschap church. Sometimes a young minister-to-be was so frightened the first time that he just did not arrive at the church on the evening he was to preach. Then Dominie Vander Werp would get up and preach to the waiting people. If this happened, the neighbor women would be watching closely when next the students came to class. Over their ironing they would wonder what the dominie had to say to the one who was afraid.

The school for ministers began as a school in the parsonage. But before the first twenty years of the church had passed, it was

more than that. On March 15, 1876, it had a real birth date, with a teacher and a place of its own.

Dominie Vander Werp was dying of cancer. He had long pleaded with the churches to call a full-time teacher. But when they called such men from the Netherlands, the men did not accept. So the students moved to Grand Rapids, where they studied with the dominie in the parsonage of the Spring Street church. To this dominie of their own, the churches sent a letter from their General Assembly meeting in Chicago in February of 1876.

They called him to be Docent of the Church, and they promised to pay him thirteen hundred dollars a year if he would provide his own house. Only a brave sacrificing man would have accepted the load of teaching at least twenty subjects to students for whom four to six years of study was high school, college, and seminary all wrapped up in one.

The General Assembly found a place for the school to meet. For fifty-two dollars a year they rented the upstairs room of the Dutch Christian School on Williams Street, a few blocks from the Spring Street church. On the day that the brave man, the Docent of the Church, Dominie Geert Egbert Boer, preached the sermon after being installed for his special work, the school began its own life. Ever since we have called March 15, 1876, its *dies natalis,* day of birth. Each year Calvin Seminary, which has come out of "the school in the upper room," holds a celebration in honor of this birthday.

FIRST CHURCHES

In their first twenty years the churches of 1857 had moved forward. They now had a school and ministers and a weekly paper. Because of these and because of God's kind favor, there was steady growing in the church then called the True Dutch Reformed Church.

In these first twenty years the four churches and one minister became thirty-two churches and seventeen ministers besides Docent Boer. The one small classis grew and was divided into four, because the churches were no longer all in Michigan. They were in seven other states, too—in New York, New Jersey, Iowa, Wisconsin, Ohio, Illinois, and Indiana.

Which churches were some of these that began in the early years?

There was the church in Pella, for one—Pella, the prairie city of seceder dominie Hendrik Pieter Scholte. To the flat grassy plains of Iowa, Scholte took eight hundred Dutchmen from the city of St. Louis where they had gathered to wait after crossing the Atlantic. These people were not as poor as the settlers in Michigan. They traveled in wagons to their new home. One oxen team pulled a wagon with the heavy iron padlocked money chest on it. At night two strong men stood guard over the chest which held the guilders of the new colony.

Dominie Scholte bought eighteen thousand acres of land on which to settle his people. After the first sod dugouts, wood was brought in to the treeless prairie. Neat homes and streets appeared. Around the houses were fences to keep out the pigs and cattle that roamed as they pleased. There was the tall-spired church where Dominie Scholte preached three-hour sermons on

100

Sunday. And on Reformation Avenue there was the home of the Scholtes, with three chimneys, nine windows across the front, some of them with little balconies. Behind the house were the formal gardens, covering several acres and laid out by landscape gardeners. These were so unusual in a new prairie settlement that people came from miles around to see them.

The house and the gardens were the dominie's effort to make his wife Mareah happy. She had learned painting and music and lived in luxury in Europe where her father was a professor. Many weeks she cried after coming to the rough cabin beside the hickory pole with the board on top which said *Pella*. From the chest of Delft dishes Mareah Scholte took with her, only six plates arrived unbroken. To comfort her, Scholte had a walk, a blue walk, made out of all the broken pieces. The walk led from the old cabin of the early months to the beautiful new home, and the Delft pieces with windmills on them were given a special place in the walk.

Pella grew fast. It was in the path of the west coast gold rush and became a thriving town, even though there were years when the fight against grasshoppers and dust seemed almost hopeless. As long as Scholte lived, his church remained independent and joined no other group. The dominie was a strong leader in many

ways. President Abraham Lincoln at one time asked him to become ambassador to Austria, but a rule was passed saying that ambassadors had to be born in the United States, and so Scholte could not accept this honor.

When Scholte died, his church died with him. While he lived, some already had left his church to join the Dutch Reformed churches. From these people, two years before the talented Dominie Scholte died, came forty-two people to make up our first church in Iowa.

The church of Oostburg was the first of our churches in Wisconsin. Oostburg lies in good land beyond the Lake Michigan port of Sheboygan. Many Dutch settlers came to this farm land, but those who arrived safely could never forget the memory of a burning ship on which one hundred twenty-seven settlers perished within sight of Sheboygan harbor.

It was in November, 1847, a year after Van Raalte first saw Black River, that the propeller steamboat *Phoenix* set out from Buffalo through the Great Lakes. Four o'clock on a Sunday morning smoke began pouring out of the engine room. The boat was badly overloaded and the night before the fire the crew had been drinking. For the four hundred passengers there were only two lifeboats, enough to save forty-three people. The fire spread. People ripped loose doors and boards and jumped with them into the icy water of the lake. The lake was quiet that night, and the Sheboygan people who gathered on the shore several miles away saw the flaming hull and the toppling masts against the blackness of the sky and the water. They sent out a lifeboat, and a propeller boat which took some time to get up enough steam to move. At seven o'clock these reached the smoldering ship and found only three people still alive in the water, clinging to their doors or boards. All the rest died in the fierce heat of the fire or

102

the icy cold of the lake. Among those saved in the two lifeboats were twenty-five Dutch settlers, who made their way sadly through the Sheboygan port to the farmlands of Oostburg and Cedar Grove.

There were other interesting churches of the first twenty years.

The church of West Sayville on Long Island, New York, was a congregation of oyster men who had learned fishing in the old country. They bought old boats cheaply and soon turned them into a valuable fleet. Each spring they planted oysters in the Great South Bay and when autumn came, they gathered them to be shipped near and far, as far as England.

In upper New York, the church at Rochester began because it was on the route which the seceders took to go west. Many stayed in Rochester where they worked at their trades and used their good gardening skill to grow vegetables which they sold to their American neighbors. Seceders stopped along their westward route in Cleveland, too, and found work in the factories. Some never went farther than Paterson and Passaic, in New Jersey. Here they joined the employees of the busy cotton and silk mills.

Others went almost all the way west, as it seemed to them then. They settled High Prairie and Low Prairie in the lowland south of Chicago. First Low Prairie, now South Holland, with its streams running into the Calumet River, its wild ducks, geese, deer, and fish, and its damp earth fertile for large vegetable farms. Then came High Prairie, now the city streets of Roseland, where once the swamp grass grew so tall that cows could not be seen as they moved about in it.

103

One seceder elder led a group across the state border into Indiana, where they called their settlement Munster after the man who was their leader. In these and other places, churches began which today can claim to be among the oldest in the Christian Reformed Church.

Ridott, Illinois, was the first German church of seceders to join the people of 1857. The border between the Netherlands and Germany had meant little to these folk, and many churches of them had joined the Dutch seceders. These German seceders also came to America, and in the early years some of their new world churches became part of us.

The number of churches in the Michigan colony grew, too, and congregations were organized in other parts of the state. In Muskegon Dutchmen worked at lumbering. The pine and hemlock logs from the forests to the north were floated down the rivers to the port of Muskegon where they were cut and shipped across Lake Michigan on their way to the prairies.

Jan Vogel, a veteran of many Civil War battles, was the Dutch seceder who explored the northwest of Michigan's peninsula, looking for cheap land because the colony was becoming crowded. With three other men, Vogel made his way north to Traverse City, where the men signed papers buying homesteads in the thick timberland of Missaukee County, sixty miles to the south. Next day they set out walking to see their new properties in the county where they were to be the first white settlers. Then they walked more than one hundred miles back to Noordeloos where they had been living. Again they set out, this time with a wagon and oxen to take their families to the spot we know as Vogel Center. Vogel called it Clam Union first, after the Clam

104

River down which the white pine logs were floated. Clam Union, deep in the lumber country, was the first of the group of churches we have today in northern Michigan.

So passed the first twenty years. God's hand had been working in the weak beginning of 1857. He brought ministers to lead and a school where others could be trained. He established churches, eight times as many as in the beginning. In one of these all-Dutch churches, on a June Sunday in 1871, a visiting minister was even invited to preach an English sermon, many years before English became the language of the Christian Reformed Church in America.

God did not do miracles. He worked through people, and so the progress was far from perfect, as the people themselves were.

But the blessing had begun. And God has been good, very good to continue the blessing through many years, even until today.

A CHURCH GROWS AND MOVES

Sometimes we take out snapshot albums to look at pictures of ourselves when we were very young. How strange it seems to see that we were once so small and different from what we are today. The same thing that happens to us has happened to our church. We who see it as it is today cannot imagine how it has grown and changed since 1857. And what would the weaver Haan and the minister Van den Bosch, who saw its birth and early years, say if they could stand with us now?

By 1956, the last year before its hundredth birthday, the Christian Reformed Church had found a place in twenty-five states, in eight Canadian provinces, in Washington, D. C., and in Alaska. It had almost five hundred churches and more than two hundred thousand members. How it grew where it was and how it reached out until it touched the Pacific Ocean and stretched from the midnight sun of Alaska to the palm trees of Florida — this is a story too long to tell, because it is a story in which each of our churches has its part. We will have to tell the story as our snapshot albums do, with word pictures taken here and there through the years.

Abraham Lincoln was campaigning to be a senator when the Christian Reformed Church was born. In the year that he was shot to death as president, the year the Civil War ended, Dominie Vander Werp began to teach students in his Graafschap parsonage.

When the Christian Reformed Church was twenty years old and thirty-two churches strong, trigger-happy hunters were still killing the last of fifteen million buffalo who roamed the western plains, and Indian tribes were in war paint, fighting to keep the white men from their hunting grounds. Alexander Graham Bell, working in Boston to teach the deaf to speak, had just invented the telephone, though no one thought this new curiosity would be very useful.

These were the years when immigrants by the millions poured into America. From every country of Europe they came, also from Holland. Among the Dutch settlers were many seceders who brought their membership to the Christian Reformed Church.

They joined our church because the Dutch seceder church had at last recognized our church of 1857. They saw that it was closer to them than the Dutch Reformed churches of America which began two centuries earlier in the east. There was especially one thing in some of these Dutch Reformed churches with which the seceder church found it could not agree. This was their belief about church members belonging to a lodge.

A lodge is a secret society, a religious organization. There are different kinds, some for men such as the Masonic Order, and some for women, like the one called Order of the Eastern Star. Each lodge has a set of secret oaths and secret ceremonies and a constitution which says certain things about God. So that anyone can join the lodge, these ideas about God are vague general ones, and nothing is said about God's son as our only Saviour. The Christian Reformed Church believes the Bible leads any true Christian to stay out of the lodges, not only because they are secret oath-taking societies, but especially because they do not believe in Jesus Christ as Saviour, even though they may try hard to do good.

Among the eastern Dutch Reformed churches, there were some members and ministers who belonged to lodges. When the Dutch seceder church discovered this, it wrote the American church about it. But the Dutch Reformed churches answered that it would be too upsetting to demand their members to leave the lodges. The seceder church turned then to the Christian Reformed Church which stood against lodge membership. When you go to America, bring your membership to the churches of 1857, said the seceder church to her people who joined the flood of immigrants leaving the Old World.

Other churches already in America asked to be added to the Christian Reformed Church because of the problem of the lodges. In the east, a group of thirteen churches who had left the Dutch Reformed Church became part of us, and were called the Classis of Hackensack. In Michigan, Van Raalte's own Holland church, with its row of stately white pillars, asked to be added to the Christian Reformed Church, and so did other churches of the middle west who wanted to stand against the lodges.

As the immigrants from the ships joined the settlers already in America, the Christian Reformed Church began to grow and move and reach new places.

The new immigrants and the earlier settlers of America pushed into the wide unclaimed lands of the west. They conquered new areas and turned them into states. This pioneering was for sturdy patient people, people willing to work and do without until they had learned the secrets of the soil and climate to which they came. All too often their troubles increased because they believed the false reports of men who wanted to make money by selling unexplored land.

The Christian Reformed Church moved westward, too, first into Kansas where the crops were good if the rain fell and the grasshoppers stayed away. Rotterdam they named the place we now know as Dispatch. Here in 1880 was the first Christian Reformed Church in Kansas, and after it came the church in Luctor. Luctor means "I struggle," and the Latin word comes from the seal of the Dutch province of Zeeland, on which there is a lion struggling to rise above the water. The early settlers of Kansas did struggle, not to push back the salty ocean but to tame the new earth and to endure the baking sun of summer and the freezing winter wind. One discouraged settler loaded his ox wagon and made the five-week trip back to Michigan from which he had come. There were more like him.

In South Dakota we had our first church six years before there was a state by this name. The beginnings were along the Platte Creek of Charles Mix county, and to the north where New Holland was the first place in Douglas county. Here too the settlers struggled. Hailstorms struck the full crops, destroying them before they could be harvested. The winters were bitter and heavy with snow, while the gentle rains of spring and summer were scarce. In one bad year, a man sold his farm of one hundred sixty acres for a hundred dollars. Some people disappeared during the night, leaving their farms and homes as payment for their heavy debts. Those who stayed through the early hard years learned to live with the drought and the storms, and slowly their living improved.

In 1886, the year the statue of liberty was set up in New York harbor, the Christian Reformed Church came to Minnesota, to the settlement called Prinsburg. Prinsburg took its name from the man Prins who with his partner Koch agreed to buy thirty-four thousand acres from the railroad for the founding of a large Dutch colony west of Minneapolis. There was so much advertising about the project that every Dutch group in America buzzed with talk of it. Not all who promised to buy acres did buy them, but Prinsburg was a beginning. In 1956 twenty-two Christian Reformed churches could be found in the state of Minnesota.

Far from the rush to the west, sixty miles out of Boston, Massachusetts, some men imported cattle for their farms from the Dutch province of Friesland. A young Dutchman came with the cattle to show the owners how to care for them. The young man urged his family and his friends to join him in America, and the coming of those people was the occasion for founding our church in Whitinsville in 1896. Sixty years later, with two hundred seventy-five families, this church was our only representative in all of New England.

In the opening year of the twentieth century we arrived at the Pacific Ocean, in the state of Washington. Lynden, a lumber town deserted after the depression of 1893, turned from a ghost town to a thriving village when Gerrit Veleke persuaded his Dutch friends from other places to settle in it. Soon the shingle factories were blowing their hundred fifty whistles again and the settlers not working in lumber started dairy and poultry farms in the steady climate of the Yakima Valley.

About Montana there were many stories. Some said the soil was salty and stony and on every summer day there was a thunderstorm, but others told of cauliflower weighing up to thirty-nine pounds. It would be more true to say that this state taught its Dutch settlers the hard way how to farm in dry soil, and when the lesson was learned, the farms prospered and the churches grew. Manhattan was the first and is still the largest of these.

The people of our Alamosa church in the Rocky Mountain area can tell how the false promises of a Dutch land agent caused the beginning of the first Christian Reformed Church in Colorado. Two hundred new settlers arrived in Alamosa, having believed the glorious stories told them. The first days they were crowded into two sheds which had been built in the open sand and sagebrush. Sick with scarlet fever and diphtheria, short of food and water, and bitter at the unkept promises of the land agent, they debated what to do. Some moved to other places, but these settlements were not successful. Those who stayed near Alamosa were the pioneers of that church which was organized in 1904, followed soon by a church in Denver, the refuge of people with lung illnesses.

110

Good climate was also the reason for our first California church in Redlands. Later came the alfalfa fields and scientific dairy farms of our people in the Bellflower and Ripon areas. Some moved to Los Angeles and began our church in that large city.

Standing at the Pacific Ocean in Washington and California, the Christian Reformed Church turned to look at some of the states it had passed by in its push to the west. To seven more of these it came before the hundred year birthday of 1957. First there was Idaho, where the beginning at a place named Amsterdam failed because enough water could not be brought into the dry fields. But Grangeville, born in 1927, has grown and is with us today.

Near to the Atlantic coastline in the state of North Carolina our first southern church sprang up. Because of slavery and the hot climate, the early Dutch settlers stayed out of the south. Many years later a man from New York persuaded a group of Dutch-Americans from other parts of the country to move to North Carolina. Here, in a place named Terra Ceia, the early spring turns the fields yellow with thousands of daffodils and narcissus, and the flower merchants of the north come down to argue over prices with the owners of the fields. What oysters and clams are to West Sayville, flowers and bulbs are to Terra Ceia. Until the churches of Florida were organized, Terra Ceia was the only southern congregation in our membership.

The second world war brought us into Washington, D. C. Among the mass of people working in the Pentagon and other government buildings were enough Christian Reformed people to make possible a church in the city where the flags of many nations fly before their embassies and the buildings of American government tower side by side for endless blocks. And since the message of our church is a message for all kinds of men, it is good that we have a voice, even though a small one, in the capital of our country.

The southwest of our country, with its dry land and mining industry, did not at first attract the Dutch settlers any more than the southern states did. Although after some years we went to New Mexico to preach to the Indians, we did not have churches in other parts of the southwest until the church of Phoenix, Arizona, was organized in 1946.

Four more states and the mushrooming territory of Alaska find their places on our list, but first comes a surprising story of ships.

All the early growing of the Christian Reformed Church could be called a story of ships, ships of Dutch people docking in the ports of a strange land. From the ships they went out to build homes and churches from the Atlantic to the Pacific. Where they settled through the years, their children also settled, and their grand-children and great-grandchildren grew up.

After fifty or sixty years the ships began to be forgotten. The Christian Reformed Church in America was growing from the inside.

But suddenly the ships appeared again. There were many of them, docking not in New York and Boston, but in Quebec and Montreal. While the forty-eight states had filled up so quickly that the United States passed laws cutting down the number of immigrants who might come in each year, the eleven provinces of the Dominion of Canada had much open land left for settlers.

As the countries of Europe began the giant task of rebuilding their bombed-out cities and factories after the second world war, people turned their eyes abroad and thought of building new homes in new places. Dutch families in the crowded war-battered country of the dikes also looked across the oceans, to Australia and New Zealand, and especially to Canada. Many of these families were from the church of the 1834 seceders, a church grown large and known as the Gereformeerde Kerken of the Netherlands.

112

The government of Canada was glad to welcome Dutch people into its provinces. In 1947 they began to arrive, their ships steaming up the broad St. Lawrence River. Now the people of 1857 had their turn to welcome and help as they had been helped a hundred years before when they were strangers to a new land and language.

The new Dutch-Canadians needed help in finding good places to settle together. They needed churches and ministers. Since they could not take much money with them out of the Netherlands, they had to struggle even to support their own families during the first years in America. Many went to the cities of Canada, while others worked for Canadian farmers until they could save enough money to buy farms of their own.

To these brothers by blood and faith came the help of the Christian Reformed Church through its home missions organization. Ministers speaking Dutch as well as English went to Canada. They did not only preach and gather new churches. They also met the boats, found houses, arranged jobs, solved problems, and acted as interpreters for the Dutch families.

Most of the money which the church set aside for home mission work during these years went to Canada, and special moneys called Canadian Emergency and Canadian Building funds were collected besides. Churches in the United States ready to buy new furnishings sent their used pews, pulpit furniture, communion sets, and Psalter Hymnals to the churches springing up in Canada.

There were never enough ministers and enough dollars to do everything that could be done. The ships arrived too fast, the new people in new places were too many. But as the flood of new settlers dropped to a smaller stream by 1955, the results of the helping could be seen.

When the churches of the Christian Reformed Church were counted early in 1956, one hundred twenty-three of them, a quarter of them all, were in Canada and could be found in eight out of the eleven Canadian provinces. More than half of these churches were in the province of Ontario, whose shoreline curves along the north of the Great Lakes and Niagara Falls. Alberta, the second province from the Pacific Ocean, stood next in line, listing churches in towns with interesting names like Red Deer, Medicine Hat, High River, and Rocky Mountain House. Edmonton, the capital of Alberta, had five Christian Reformed churches, the largest number in any one Canadian city. In British Columbia, its coast of many fingers washed by the Pacific Ocean, the third largest group of our churches could be found.

It is interesting that the Christian Reformed Church in Canada did not begin with the ships after the second world war. More than forty years earlier, people from our Montana churches crossed the border into Alberta and began a church there in 1905. They suffered and struggled through the first years just as new settlers did on the frontiers of the United States. First they lived in holes with branches over the top for a roof. It is said that one man harnessed himself to his buggy because he had no horse to pull it into town for supplies. Another man turned a table upside down and pushed it along the railroad tracks to carry provisions to his new farm.

The churches of western Canada were hard to reach and they often went without ministers for a long time. The plucky church of Burdett in Alberta got along forty-four years with elders reading sermons and students preaching a few summers before it finally received its first minister in 1955.

When the ships began to dock in 1947 there were only fourteen churches in Canada, six of them in the province of Alberta. By 1956 the number had leaped from fourteen to one hundred twenty-three, from less than five hundred families to almost eight thousand of them. The hard years were behind them, and the Christian Reformed churches of Canada were fast growing and thriving on the new continent to which most of their people had lately come.

In the five years after 1950 we made our way into four more states and into Alaska. Three churches began in Florida's fast-growing cities and vacationland. In Pennsylvania, the work went on in Philadelphia, Benjamin Franklin's city of brotherly love. Strangely, we had been in both these states once long before but these beginnings had disappeared. Oklahoma City and Salt Lake City were in two states new to us. When we came to these, we could count churches in just over half the states of the nation. Much had been done, but there was still that other half, challenging us.

When the United States set up its army outposts in Alaska, Christian Reformed boys were among the servicemen assigned to these camps of the far north. Through their enthusiasm the church to which they belonged began to speak in the modern cities of Anchorage and Fairbanks. A minister was ready to face the work in this new frontier. Two buildings were completed by the members in the season when the midnight sun added hours of light to the day. With this brave start, our church began its work and preaching. It looked forward to the day when it would reach not only servicemen but also many among the teeming thousands who have come to Alaska to stay, as well as the Eskimo natives whose dog sleds and igloos are the part of Alaska we have always known.

❊   ❊   ❊   ❊   ❊

In the spring of 1857 a few men from a few churches sat in the hill church of Graafschap and called themselves a classis, the first classis of a new church. God blessed that new church, adding to it many Dutch-Americans who lived in the cities and farmlands of America. He even began to add to it some of our neighbors who are Americans with us, though they trace their families back to other countries of the Old World.

It was 1896, the year Thomas Edison received a patent for inventing the radio, when church one hundred was established. In the year 1912, on a quiet moonlit night, God sent an iceberg to sink the luxury liner *Titanic* as she crossed the Atlantic on her

116

first voyage. Every headline told the news of fifteen hundred drownings, and for a time men remembered not to boast as loudly about what they could do. This was the year, though the news made no headlines, that the Christian Reformed Church welcomed church two hundred into its membership.

In 1940 the war machine of Adolph Hitler was rolling, crushing Norway, Denmark, Belgium and the Netherlands, breaking through to conquer France, battering Britain's island fortress with waves of bombers. In this unforgettable year we counted church three hundred.

Then it was 1952, with the killing of war still fresh in the earth. Dwight Eisenhower was in his first year as president, and across the Pacific in Korea the truce teams of the Communists and the United Nations met and deadlocked in the tents of Panmunjon. Church four hundred, said the yearbook, had been born among us.

And as the hundredth year came into view, it was almost time to welcome church five hundred into the growing family called Christian Reformed.

THE WALL COMES DOWN

In America, the giant melting pot where English and Scotch-Irish, German and Italian mixed together into one people, the Dutch of the Christian Reformed Church melted and mixed slowly.

For many years they hoped they would not need to melt and mix at all. By settling together in colonies, they planned to keep intact their churches and schools and their whole way of Christian living. We will lose what is precious to us if we do not stay together and by ourselves, they said.

The spire of the church marked the center of living in the colonies. Twice on Sundays the wagons and buggies arrived at the church from all around. Reading the church papers and going to church meetings, and talking of all these things over a cup of coffee and a slice of homemade bread — this filled the hours after work throughout the week. It was as if each settlement lived within a wall, the wall of Dutch language and Dutch living. The wall cut them off from those around, and little came in or went out through it. When the colonies grew, the walls grew with them and went on protecting them well.

But then the children born within the wall grew up. In the cities they went to work in factories and offices, where they moved among their neighbors beyond the wall. These children began to say to their fathers, Why must we speak in the tongue of the old land? We are in America, and its language is for us.

But the fathers shook their heads and told the impatient younger generation to be still and to wait. They did not see then that the wall had already begun to break down.

In the spring of 1887, thirty years after the beginning of the Christian Reformed Church, eighteen people banded together to form the first English-speaking congregation, the church we know today as the LaGrave Avenue church in Grand Rapids. Many were against such a church. It is a rash move, they said, and who knows whether it will not bring trouble, and a split among the churches?

To such people it seemed that keeping a pure church meant also keeping a Dutch church. And they were not wrong when they pointed to the safety and blessing of the early years within the wall. But the new generation also spoke the truth when it said, We cannot ourselves become Americans while we keep our church Dutch.

118

A few years later a group of churches in the east asked to come into the Christian Reformed Church. We called them Classis Hackensack. These churches had been speaking the English language for more than a century. They sang hymns as well as psalms in their worship, and they published an English weekly paper called *The Banner of Truth*.

From these churches, while they were still the True Protestant Reformed Dutch Church, came the first English-speaking minister of the Christian Reformed Church. He was the Reverend John Y. De Baun, called to be pastor at the LaGrave church. He also gave the first books to begin a library in our theological school.

Publishing of *The Banner of Truth* was moved to Grand Rapids and in 1914 the church bought this weekly to be its official English church paper. The Christian Reformed Church places great value on the written word. It has long had its own publishing plant where *De Wachter, The Banner*, Sunday School papers, and many tracts are printed. Today these papers roll off the presses in our new denominational building where the publishing house and mission boards have their modern offices.

When the churches of Classis Hackensack sent their men to synod after 1890, they could not understand the Dutch spoken by men of the other classes. So synod translated the motions into English for the Hackensack men. More and more the two languages began to be used side by side. It was Dutch and English in the church papers, the Sunday school lessons, the church catechism classes, and the Christian schools.

But this double language could not last forever, though it did last until the church was eighty years old. As the early immigrants passed away, their English-speaking children and grandchildren stood in their places.

In 1914 came the first world war. The United States crossed an ocean to fight, and her troops were fiercely proud to be Americans. In Iowa, where we have the second largest group of our churches, the governor ordered no foreign language spoken at public meetings. In the trenches of Europe and on the streets at home, people rallied behind the stars and stripes and forgot the countries from which their forefathers had come.

These war years tipped the scales in favor of the English language in Christian Reformed churches and it weighed more heavily year by year. Yet it went slowly, not all at once. In 1937 there were still a few reports in Dutch for the synod.

The spread of the English language did not mark the end of the wall. Though we had taken on the speech of the land in which we lived, we had not yet given out and shared the distinctive faith and the way of life which were precious to us.

The Christian Reformed Church did not quickly take down this part of the wall. For many years its mission work at home was among new Dutch immigrants and among the American Indians whom it called "the heathen" of our country. Then came the beginning of the work in South America, China, and Africa. Still the church at home, speaking English, was a church of Dutch-Americans only.

In 1939 the church decided to speak by radio voice. Over the air came the first messages from our church to the people of America. We were beginning to scatter the seed. Later years would see us ready to bring in the American harvest.

Another war came first. Though it brought sorrow and death all over the world, it brought to us more challenge to lay low the wall. Twenty-five Christian Reformed ministers put on chaplains' uniforms and served all over the world. They saw at first hand the power of the Gospel as we try faithfully to preach it.

The rest of our servicemen saw it, too. They were in the deserts of North Africa where the Mohammedans kneel four times a day to the east, with their faces to the ground. They walked among the gorgeous buildings of the church of Rome. In the Pacific they saw the shrines and idols of the Buddhist and Shinto faiths.

Far from home, they also learned to know their American neighbors better. In the barracks and the mess halls, on landing craft and jungle marches, under fire and on leave, the servicemen of the Christian Reformed Church served with all kinds of Americans. They saw them die with God and they saw them die without him. If they thought at all, they began to prize the faith they had been taught, and they ceased to be ashamed of it. Through the letters without stamps that filled the mailman's bag during the years of World War II, the people at home also saw more clearly the needs of those outside the wall.

In the last ten years new names have begun to appear among the long lists of those which begin with De and Van and end with -stra and -ma. Among our ministers there are such names as Callender, McLeod, Licatesi, and Jen. Some churches list families with names like Aufiero, Brown, Campbell, Markey, Mesaros, O'Brien, Scott, Skala, and Wu.

These names are a sign of what is happening at last to the Dutch wall. In the early years we needed the wall. It sheltered us well and gave us time to grow stronger. But today we are no longer a church walled in. The Christian Reformed Church is a church on the march.

MR. CHRISTIAN REFORMED

During the years when the wall was breaking down, there was one man especially who never tired of speaking and working for our church. Some called him Mr. Christian Reformed, because they only knew of our church through him. The Queen of the Netherlands made him a knight, Muskingum College of the Presbyterians made him a doctor, and an Encyclopedia of Michigan gave him a place in its pages.

While the Christian Reformed Church of America was almost unknown, the Reverend Doctor Sir Henry Beets was among her best spokesmen, not only at home but also in many places where he traveled abroad.

He was a short, stocky man, whose wiry black hair and full mustache turned white. His voice had a kind of nasal twang and he spoke slowly, with force and with well-rolled r's. Wherever he went he was full of questions. The answers he stored away in his mind or in his little black notebooks, and he made good use of them later on.

Henry Beets was born the son of a farmer in the little town of Koedijk on the peninsula of North Holland which lay below the level of the North Sea. He remembered it happily as a place where "the dunes are brightly yellow, and the grass is deeply green, the dikes high and the canals broad."

His mother, a faithful member of the church of the seceders, died when her son Henry was young. The new stepmother had no use for the psalms and prayers the boy had learned. Once she found him kneeling beside his bed and she teased him about his "fine tricks."

When he grew up, Henry left the Netherlands to join the family of his mother's brother in Luctor, Kansas. On the fourth of July,

when he was seventeen years old, the young immigrant stepped from the gangplank into his new country. Henry had taught himself English, as well as French and German, while he was still in Koedijk, so he went swiftly through the grades in the white schoolhouse near Luctor.

After the years in his father's house where Christ had been a stranger, Henry Beets was in a new world spiritually, too. Eagerly he heard the preaching of traveling missionaries or the Spurgeon sermons read by the elders. He sang again the psalms his mother had loved and he read his Dutch Bible carefully. After professing his faith before the church, he made plans to study for the ministry at the theological school in Grand Rapids, Michigan.

As a minister of the Christian Reformed Church, the Reverend Henry Beets was a man of many firsts. He was first full-time director of missions, for twenty years, after being secretary of the Board of Missions for twenty-five years. He was first editor of *The Banner,* for twenty-five years. He was first stated clerk of synod, preparing and keeping the papers of the synod for forty years.

Henry Beets did more. Epecially he wrote — articles, catechism books, poetry, and many books, books of sermons and meditations. He wrote books in Dutch about American presidents to tell the immigrants about these great men. He wrote books, many of them, about the history and the missions of the Christian Reformed Church. No one knew the story of that church better than Sir Henry did. Because he wrote it for us, the story has not been lost.

Doctor Beets traveled, too, in a day when many people did not travel as they do today. Five times he was in the Netherlands, speaking for our church at the Dutch general synods. Three times he went to South America, and once he went around the world because of his interest in missions. Wherever he went, people met the Christian Reformed Church when they met Henry Beets.

Each time he came back to his home on Madison Avenue in Grand Rapids and sat down before the Delft tiles that framed his fireplace, planning what he would do next to make his church better known and more active. To make that church a real part of America — this was his aim.

By his pen and by his tongue Henry Beets made a place for the church he loved. The Christian Reformed Church has a lasting place in her heart for him, too.

WE WORSHIP

America is full of churches. But not many of them are full churches. They have long lists of members whom they rarely see. There are many empty benches when the ministers stand to preach on Sunday mornings. The Sunday evening worship has quite disappeared.

This is not true of the Christian Reformed Church. God has kept her a full church. Except for the sick and those away from home, the people whose names appear on the membership rolls of the church are sitting in its pews to worship on Sunday. Whole families of them are there, beginning and ending the Lord's day in the Lord's house. It does not take Easter or Christmas or some other special day to bring them. Rain, sleep, callers, golf, and gardening do not keep them away.

The people of this full church worship much after the way of the early church. Perhaps the minister dresses differently, in a robe or before that in a formal cutaway suit. The language is English, the place America, but the worship has come down through the ages and is not changed by these outward things.

The people praise God. They confess their sins to him and he forgives them through the blood of his Son. God speaks to his people from his Word, teaching them. This message the preacher brings in his sermon, and it is the high point of the worship. From the beginning of Christ's church it has been so. The Reformation put this Word of God back into its right place again, and took away all the fancy trimmings that had robbed it of its glory.

Every Sunday the people bring their sacrifices. They offer their hearts anew and they give their money to be used in the work of the church. Some Sundays they celebrate the perfect sacrifice of Christ in a special way. Beneath the snowy linen cloths the bread and wine of the Lord's Supper lie in their silver dishes. Today there are usually tiny glasses for the wine instead of a large cup passed from one to another. But the meaning of the Lord's Supper is the same always.

Christ in his body is not in the bread and wine, as some teach, or with it, as others say. He is there, to be sure, but in a spiritual way. Through this earthly food, which he himself commanded, we remember his body and blood given on the tree of the cross for us. Only those reverently stretch out their hands to take the bread and wine who have confessed Christ before the church.

I baptize thee into the name of the Father, and of the Son, and of the Holy Spirit, Amen. There are two sacraments of the church of Christ, and these are the words of the second, holy baptism. The minister speaks them as he dips his hand into water and sprinkles it on the head of a new baby. There is no magic power in baptism, and the water is not holy. But when parents bring their little children to receive this sign from God, God tells them and he tells the congregation watching that his promise to Abraham has continued through all centuries to believing parents of today. Sometimes that promise comes for the first time when a person is full-grown. Then the water of baptism falls on his bowed head while he kneels after standing to make his own confession of his newly found Lord.

What a holy thing it is to worship the Lord in his house, by the praising and confessing, the preaching and the sacrificing, and by the holy sacraments Christ has given to his church.

THIS WE BELIEVE

In the pew racks of our churches a maroon covered book stands beside the Bible. This is the *Psalter Hymnal,* as the gold letters on its cover tell. It is the official praise book of the Christian Reformed Church. In it are more of the unchanged treasures which the Christian Reformed Church holds dear.

First there are the psalms set to music, still sung in our churches as they have been sung for hundreds of years in many languages and in many lands. After the psalms come a smaller number of choice hymns.

The last part of the book is not of music. It holds the famous creeds by which the Christian Reformed Church says what it believes about the Bible and about what God teaches us in it. There are especially three of these creeds, or doctrinal standards.

Everyone in the Christian Reformed Church agrees to them when he becomes a full member of the church. Ministers, professors, elders and deacons sign their names to a Form of Subscription in which they promise to teach and defend the Word of God and the creeds of the church. There is no going back on this sacred promise. In its hundred-year history, the Christian Reformed Church has removed a seminary professor and several ministers who at different times would not stop teaching and preaching what the church believed to be contrary to God's Word as it is set forth in the standards.

The first standard comes to us from what is now Belgium and it is called the Belgic Confession. When it was written in 1561, during the years of the great Reformation, Belgium was still the southern part of the Netherlands. Its government, following the church of Rome, fiercely persecuted the Reformed followers of John Calvin.

One of the Reformed preachers, Guido de Brés, wrote this confession of faith for almost the same reason that Calvin first wrote his *Institutes*. He sent a copy to King Philip to explain what the persecuted Reformed Christians believed and to show that they were not lawless rebels. In the letter to the king that was sent with the Confession, De Brés said that he and the Christians with him would "offer their backs to stripes, their tongues to knives, their mouths to gags, and their whole bodies to the fire," but they would not forsake God's truth as set forth in the Confession.

Preacher de Brés did give his whole body for his faith. He died a martyr six years after writing the Confession. But it has lived on and its thirty-seven articles are a lasting treasure of the church of Jesus Christ.

The second standard of the Christian Reformed Church is the one we know best. Every Sunday our ministers must use it as a guide to explaining the Bible in an orderly and thorough way. This Heidelberg Catechism has been translated into all the languages of Europe and many languages of Asia.

It appeared two years after the Belgic Confession, and a year before John Calvin died. A professor and a court preacher wrote it together. They took some of their ideas from a catechism written by a Polish nobleman who fled to London and became minister of a church of religious refugees there.

Frederick III, called an Elector, ordered the catechism written. From his palace in the picturesque town of Heidelberg beside the Rhine River, he ruled over one of the German provinces. He was eager to have the Reformed faith become the belief of his people. So he asked Caspar Olevianus, his court preacher, and Zacharias Ursinus, a university professor, to write a catechism which could be used for teaching the people.

The Heidelberg Catechism was a success at once. Three extra editions were printed in the first year. We know the Catechism as divided into fifty-two parts, called Lord's Days. This dividing was done at the time of the third printing so that the Catechism could be used for preaching, too, one part for each Sunday of the year.

From the teaching of the Frenchman Calvin, influenced by the Polish nobleman in England, written by two men of Germany, adopted by the great Dutch Synod of Dort, and transplanted to the new world where the church of 1857 was born — down this path of four hundred years come the questions and answers of the Heidelberg Catechism to a church which still holds fast to what the Catechism teaches from the full Word of God.

That famous synod of the Reformed churches, the Synod of Dort, gave us our third standard. The synod began in the year 1618, more than fifty years after the court preacher and the professor wrote their Catechism. For six months the meetings went on in a long recreation hall of the Dutch town called Dort, or Dordrecht. At the end of this time, the Dutch delegates and the twenty-seven delegates from other countries were ready to present five large articles of faith to the Reformed churches from which they came. These are called the Canons of Dort.

The men who sat around the big center table and at the desks on the sides of the gymnasium faced a serious problem. They had been called together to decide what to do about the teachings of an orphan who had grown up to become a brilliant professor of theology in the University of Leyden. With all his genius, this professor named Arminius had been teaching his students certain doctrines contrary to the Reformed faith. The students spread them in the churches where they became ministers, and soon there was a struggle between the followers of Arminius and those who still held to the truths of the Reformed faith. Even though

Arminius himself died nine years before the Synod of Dort, his doctrines were still very much alive and spreading.

Arminius took his own stand on five important points. Those who followed him were called Arminians, and even today the name is sometimes used by those who follow the Canons of Dort when they speak of those who do not.

God chooses to be saved men whom he knows will decide for themselves to believe, said Arminius. By so doing he struck a blow at the Bible teaching of election, which says that God does all the choosing.

Arminius also said Jesus died for everyone. By so saying the Leyden professor opposed the Reformed view that although Jesus' sacrifice was great enough to cover everyone, he died only for those whom God leads to believe. Arminius also taught that men are only partly bad, that if they wish they can stand against the grace of God when it is sent into their souls, and that it is up to men whether they will persevere in the faith after they truly believe.

The Synod of Dort stood firmly against these five errors. It wrote a section, or canon, on each one. Every canon has two parts. First it states what the Synod of Dort believes from the Word of God. Then it lists exactly the error of Arminius and argues against it. Besides its own document, the Synod of Dort voted to make the Belgic Confession and the Heidelberg Catechism the official standards of the Reformed churches.

From these churches, almost two hundred fifty years later, the Christian Reformed Church of America also took as its cornerstones of faith the Confession, the Catechism, and the Canons.

Turning the pages of the *Psalter Hymnal,* we find three more creeds. They are called ecumenical because they have been used by all churches, not only by those called Reformed. These creeds are very old, coming from the early years after Pentecost. They are small, and priceless in their beauty and thought.

I believe in God the father Almighty . . . . Together we recite the Apostolic Creed, born out of the apostles' teachings in the early church. We study it as a part of the Heidelberg Catechism.

God of God, Light of Light, very God of very God . . . . This is a line of the Nicene Creed, almost singing its way along, defending Christ as wholly and truly God. It is a creed coming from a general council called by the Emperor Constantine. Three hundred bishops arrived at his gorgeous palace in the little waterfront town of Nicaea near Constantinople. Is Jesus Christ completely God and therefore able to save us from sin, or is he not? Indeed, Christ is "very God of very God . . . of one substance with the Father" proclaimed the council meeting in the great hall of the palace in the year 325 after Christ.

There are not three almighties, but one almighty. This is the creed called Athanasian speaking about the trinity of God. It is named after Athanasius of the church of Alexandria, the leader of those who called Christ very God at the Council of Nicaea.

Although we no longer believe that Athanasius wrote this creed, it remains a gem of the church as it speaks especially about God being three in one, and about Christ being both human and divine. In the Roman churches, which calls themselves the Catholic churches, this creed is chanted in Latin on certain special days.

The *Psalter Hymnal* ends with the liturgy of the Christian Reformed Church. Here are prayers from Calvin's times which may be used in church or at home. Here are the forms, the written words, which must be used in the church for the sacraments. There is a form for weddings and one for making public pro-

131

fession of faith. These we hear often through the years. Less often and sadly we hear the reading of the form which puts a member out of the church because he will not turn from continued sinning. Sometimes the minister can read with joy the form which takes such a person back into the church later, if he truly repents and lives differently.

Officers of the church are installed into their sacred work with words written for such occasions. These too are found in the last pages of the *Psalter Hymnal*. Ministers, elders and deacons, missionaries, professors of the seminary—as servants of Christ and his church, each answers firmly to the questions asked of him, "I do, with all my heart."

CARING FOR SOULS

Many churches care for the poor and the sick. Many churches take care to build beautiful useful buildings. But not all of them give the same care to the souls of their members for which they must answer to Christ. This caring for souls is a special concern of the Christian Reformed Church.

Of course our church cares for bodies and buildings, too. It helps the poor and the sick and gives a regular pension to retired ministers or to their widows. When floods or fires or tornadoes strike one church, all the others are ready to help. New churches can borrow money for their buildings and ask help in paying their minister's salary until they have grown enough to take care of these things for themselves.

Caring for souls comes besides all this. It begins early. Children of the church come for a class every week with their minister. For ten years they study about the Bible and about their church. Besides what they learn in the Christian school and at home and on Sunday, these classes make them ready to take a stand for Christ, as the Lord leads them.

When the minister rings the doorbell, he comes as a special visitor. He comes regularly to every family of his church, bringing an elder with him. This is part of caring for souls, too. We call it family visiting. The minister and the elder come to pray with the father and mother and children. How are you living and working for Christ in your home and your work? they ask. What are you doing to help in the life of the church? In love they ask and they point the way to serving the Lord better. Family visiting is an honored Dutch custom, kept by the Christian Reformed Church in America. It brings blessing, both to the families at home and to the larger family of the church.

133

Sometimes caring for souls means punishing and even removing them from the church if they do not want to be faithful to Christ. This we call church discipline. It is a slow patient way of warning and praying over and over again. Finally, if the member will not listen and repent, he must be taken from the membership of the church, to teach him and to keep the church pure for Christ, its head.

Everything here on earth changes. Only God never changes, nor does the Word that he has given us. Many churches have made the mistake of changing what God says and what he is. They make him more like themselves, and so they often lose him. If the Christian Reformed Church is sometimes slow to make good changes on the outside, it is because she wants to guard so carefully against any changes in the things that really matter.

In a world that changes, the Christian Reformed Church prays to be true to the God and to the Word that are forever the same.

134

THE SCHOOL OF THE CHURCH

In the upstairs rented hall of the Dutch school on Williams Street, Professor Boer stood before his students. For seven years he alone had been teaching them. Every year there were more students for whom Professor Boer was high school and college and seminary. Most of the ministers-to-be attended school six years in that upper room before they went to serve their first churches.

Then synod gave the overburdened teacher a helper. Dominie Gerrit Klaas Hemkes taught part-time for the first year, and came in every week from his church in Vriesland. It was a long trip in those days to come the sixteen miles from the Vriesland church to the Williams Street school. "Monday mornings the train arrived at Vriesland Station at six o'clock in the morning," said Professor Hemkes, telling about those trips later. "But Vriesland Station is not Vriesland Church. The sticky clay was bad for a buggy and bad for a cutter. So I walked the three miles in the dark. Sometimes I missed the train. Then I waited for the freight, was held up for an hour at Hudsonville, a half hour at Jenison, and quite a while at Grandville. About noon I stumbled into my classroom."

A third professor, the young and talented Dr. Geerhardus Vos, also came to teach in the upper room. He was the first to teach the English language and he used it in all his classes. We lost much when he left to become a professor at Princeton Seminary, but by his going we had also begun to give something of ourselves to the world outside our small Dutch circle.

It took faith to see ahead in those early days of the school, when three professors made the upper room too small. By faith the church chose a good piece of land, away from the middle of the town, on the corner of Madison and Franklin.

By sacrifice the people of the church built on that land a building of stone and red brick, two stories tall, with a sort of tower in one corner and a long flight of cement steps leading up to the double wooden doors. On the stone in front of the school were these words: Theological School of the Holland Christian Reformed Church, Erected by the Grace of God, A.D. 1891.

Some said of the new school, It is too big. We will never fill it. But others, looking farther, said, Now we have room also for our young people who want to study for other work than the ministry. Let them, too, be taught in our school.

And a few, to whom the Lord gave a far look, saw even beyond the new building. They saw the theological school of the church becoming a complete college as well as a seminary. And beyond, they glimpsed the glory of a Calvinistic university.

Perhaps if we of today's church are willing to trust and to sacrifice as did the early followers of 1857, we shall see it in our day — that university rising from its dream to be the crown of all our Christian education.

SILVER, GOLD, AND DIAMOND

The people came through a light snowfall to the school on Madison and Franklin. They were gathering to celebrate a special birthday. It was March 15, 1901, twenty-five years since Dominie Boer had preached his inaugural address when the school had its beginning. Now the faculty numbered seven, the students seventy. This was the silver jubilee.

There were thirteen speeches that night. Among them were the words of Dominie Noordewier who had gone up and down the country collecting money from the churches for the new school

137

which had cost twenty-eight thousand dollars. "One man asked me whether I had the gumption to try collecting such a big sum of money," he told the audience. "I said I thought the Lord would provide." No one sitting there that night doubted that he had.

The Lord had provided also the beginnings of a college. There were two departments in the school at the time of the silver jubilee. The literary department was for all, and its courses lasted four years. The ministers-to-be called it their prep school and they graduated from it into the second department, the theological department, which was only for them.

Soon the literary department was called the Academy. Slowly, surely, the college rose from the Academy. First, two years were added with more professors and the name John Calvin Junior College. And then in 1920 the other two years to make the school all of a college, Calvin College, in addition to the three years of seminary.

But now the big new building of 1891 had become too small. Even with the theological classes in the afternoon and the literary classes in the morning, even with the adding of another piece to the building, it was not enough. And so the Academy became the Christian High School of Grand Rapids, given over into the hands of an association of parents. Calvin College and Seminary moved on to larger quarters.

This time it was not just a corner. The land was ten acres, a large block in the best suburbs of Grand Rapids. In 1916, near the end of the first world war, the cornerstone was laid and the red brick building went up, with four tall pillars across the front portico and a white spire against the blue sky.

This is very large, we said of the new building standing in the center of the ten acres. In it were classrooms and laboratories,

138

library and office space, and a high-ceilinged chapel to seat seven hundred fifty people. It stood there at the milestone of the golden jubilee, and the Christian Reformed Church thanked God for this new sign of blessing.

More cornerstones were laid in the years that followed. In 1923 it was the dormitory with its gymnasium. This was a men's dorm, except for the years of the second world war when the men were away fighting, and the girls lived in the rooms on the three floors.

In 1928 the first library went up, with a small white spire to match the large one on the main building. In 1930 the seminary moved to a new building, a home of its own.

The second world war ended and suddenly the campus was full of students, veterans coming back to study with all the others. The buildings on the ten acres were full, brimming over. But there was still room to build two more, the million dollar science building and the commons where students could eat and lounge and hold meetings. A row of houses across Franklin Street was bought to provide homes for many of the out-of-town girls. The library received a large new wing so it could hold the sixty thousand books, seven thousand phonograph records, and the four hundred magazines that come in regularly.

So came the year of diamond jubilee, of seventy-five years growing. Seventy professors now, as many professors as there were students at the time of the silver jubilee. Fifteen hundred students studying the arts and sciences, twice as many as the chapel would hold. In the seminary some of the classes took turns using the upstairs assembly room because the regular classrooms were too small.

Who had thought the problem would come again? Now the ten acres were too small. Perhaps there was a little more ground, a

139

few more houses that could be bought for a price within the sound of the carillon chiming the hours from the white spire. But if God continued to bless Calvin College and Seminary, the campus, with all that could be added from around it, would be as small as the square brick building on Madison and the upstairs room on Williams had also become too small in their day.

The synod of 1956 rode in a caravan of cars to see a new piece of property, still farther out in the southeast suburbs of Grand Rapids. Not a corner or ten acres this time, but a hundred sixty acres of estate and rolling fields.

We will buy it, said the synod, and we will study carefully how to use the new land wisely, how best to build for the Calvin of tomorrow.

THE SAME FOUNDATION

Few of us remember the school in the upper room, and those who graduated from it have also graduated from their life on earth.

Some of us remember the dark wooden stairs to the basement of the Madison building, and the chain and padlock that fastened the outside double doors when the school day was over.

Others of us remember going in and out between the tall white pillars, passing the chapel doors and the statue of Moses which had a strange way of disappearing now and then.

Some of us, still looking ahead to Calvin days, may walk in newer halls and sleep in lovelier dormitories and worship in a chapel where all the student body can find a place.

But it will be the same school, God blessing it, no matter where it stands or how many faculties and students it counts. For it has the same foundation today that gave strength to the school in the rented room on Williams Street.

God himself is that foundation, and Christ is the chief corner-stone. All our knowledge comes from him. He is first and at the center of everything man can learn. And so all learning must begin with him, or it is not true learning. It must be the very best education or it is not worthy of him.

This kind of education Calvin College and Seminary must give. They must lead in our Christian thinking and writing. They must give us leaders — ministers and missionaries, Christian teachers and doctors and nurses. Through our school we must give something to the world — men of science, discovering new things, men to sit on judges' benches and men to stand before classes in the colleges and universities of the nation. We give something also through the foreign students who study with us, returning to their homes with the learning and the spirit of our school.

Calvin College and Seminary take their name from the great reformer who set up his own schools in Geneva. John Calvin showed the world anew that every part of life must do glory to God.

This is Calvinism, that God is supreme in every field, in all that man can learn. This, God helping us, is also Calvin College and Calvin Seminary—and Calvin University to be.

THROUGH THE PEOPLE OF THE CHURCH

When Dominie Van Raalte started his Dutch colony in the woods along the Black River, he had many hopes for it. One of them was the hope of Christian schools for the children of the church. In the Netherlands the seceders had not been free to have their own schools. But the settlers of the colony soon seemed to forget the Christian schools for which they had come, even though Van Raalte often pleaded for them to be set up.

Some of the settlers who came to Van Raalte's colonies did not forget. Even though they left his church in 1857, they took his hope with them. It was their hope, too. If Van Raalte could stand with us today, he would see how Christian Reformed people have made the Christian School come true in a way he never dreamed.

We could show him hundreds of Christian schools, grade schools and high schools, gathered together into a National Union of Christian Schools. They are not schools of the church, as Calvin College and Seminary are. They belong to the Christian parents of our churches and of other churches who have followed our leading.

The parents pay for the schools and take charge of them. The churches help in every way they can. Together they work for schools where God is the center from the very beginning. Like the three legs on a tripod, the Christian home and the Christian church and the Christian school must stand together.

The people of our church have done other things which should not be forgotten. They have formed themselves into groups and started Christian hospitals for those whose minds are ill or feeble. There is Pine Rest in Michigan, Goffle Hill in the east, and

Bethesda in the west. The deacons of the churches have taken a special part in the works of Christian mercy. Often our people work together with friends of the Reformed Church whom time and a like faith have brought close to us again.

The people of the church make possible Elim School for children who are blind or deaf or crippled. They support the Children's Retreat for retarded children whose minds are not up to the level of others. Bethany Home is a happy home for children from broken families. There are homes for the old and rest homes for those long sick. There are special agencies to give Christian counseling for problems and to help with adopting children into Christian homes.

All this is not really the story of our church itself. But it is good to know that the love of Christ shines out through the people of the churches, who remember how Christ gave special love and care to those who needed it when he was on earth.

And our people remember the value Jesus put on such loving care of others when he said, "Verily I say unto you, Inasmuch as ye have done it unto one of the least of these my brethren, ye have done it unto me."

144

TO THOSE WHO DO NOT KNOW

On the last day of September in 1896 people from all the Christian Reformed churches in Grand Rapids gathered in the church building on Spring Street. It was a large building with a gallery on three sides, and this made it a good place for special gatherings. On this special evening the organist played, the audience waited, and presently the door of the little room behind the pulpit was opened from the inside. Out marched a line of sober-faced men in black Prince Albert suits. The last of these men was young, almost too young for such a dignified outfit. With him walked his young wife and behind them came another young man in a business suit and his bride, who was a nurse.

Something important was happening in the Christian Reformed Church that evening, something even more important than the people filling every seat could realize. This was the beginning of our bringing Christ to people who do not know him. It was the successful beginning of our Indian and foreign missions work.

In a service of singing and prayer and Scripture and two sermons, a seminary graduate was being installed as missionary to American Indians. Herman Fryling knelt while all the ministers in the church laid their hands upon his bowed head, and the people sang with a mighty voice, *Dat's Heeren zegen op U daal,* Jehovah's blessing on your task.

FIRST FIELD

Ten days later the new missionary Fryling with his wife and
missionary helpers, the Andrew Vander Wagens, stood on the
station platform in Gallup, New Mexico. The Sante Fe train
which had brought them from Chicago puffed on its way farther
west and disappeared down the track.

Gallup is a kind of gateway to the Navajo Indian reservation,
though the reservation covers sixteen million acres and reaches
into three states. Through that gateway the four young missionaries set out for a place on the reservation called Fort Defiance.
It was to the north and just across the border in Arizona, a place
where the white man had set up his fort while he fought down

the Navajos. At Fort Defiance the Christian Reformed Church was arranging to buy some mission buildings from the Methodists for nine hundred dollars.

This country, high above sea level, was new and strange to the four missionaries. Cactus and sagebrush and pinion trees took root in the dry earth. Steep arroyos turned into wild rushing torrents after a rainstorm. Coyotes and rattlesnakes made their homes among the rocks.

The Navajos to whom the missionaries had come were a tribe of sheep herders and goat herders. Their round hogan homes, made of logs covered with earth, were scattered all over the reservation. Summers the men and boys drove their herds higher into the hills and made their homes in three-sided lean-to huts of branches. From the wool of the sheep came yarns for the weaving looms, brightly dyed to make blankets and rugs. From the hide of the sheep came leather, finely tooled into saddle bags and belts.

These were people with a language of their own, a hard language for the white man to master. They worshiped their own gods with many ceremonies, begging healing and rain and good harvest by wild dances and sacrifices and paintings in the sand. The Navajos were superstitious, afraid of many evil spirits, slaves to the queer brews and chants of their medicine men.

And there was something more, a hatred the Navajo shared with all his Indian brothers of other tribes. The red men hated the white man. They hated him for the rifle bullets and the false promises with which he had pushed them back and fenced them in. The red men hated the white man for the proud harsh ways by which he had made himself master from the Atlantic to the Pacific.

For his part, the white man felt a little guilty about what he had done to the first citizens of America. The government of the white man gave the red men land, acres of it, where they could live alone. The red men took the land. They had been beaten in war, so what else could they do? Still feeling somewhat guilty, the white man went on giving, goods and money and schools. The red men found a new way to show their anger. They became lazy and let the white man take care of them.

Soon missionaries came from different kinds of churches in America. They brought the Indians another kind of gift, the news of the true God. To them the red men acted as they did to the government. They took what they wished from the missions and the missionaries. But they accepted neither the white man nor the white man's God. The old anger was hidden behind stony faces, but it had not gone away.

To such people the Christian Reformed Church had decided to come. Elder Kniphuizen of Grand Haven had the idea first from a book he had been reading. Dominie J. H. Vos kept the Indian before the people of the church until the synod was ready to say, Yes, these are the heathen of our own land. We owe them a debt. Let our first missionaries be sent to the Indians.

But which Indians? And where? The first try was a failure. One missionary went in 1889 to South Dakota, to the Sioux Indians on the Rosebud Reservation. He found a schoolhouse to use and told the Indians nearby that he would meet them there on Sunday. But no Indian came on Sunday, though the missionary waited a long time. Lonely and discouraged after weeks of trying this method, he gave up.

And so the cause of Indian missions waited. It waited for men willing to be missionaries, and for synod to decide where to send them.

The four missionaries at Fort Defiance were the real beginning of the work which has been carried on for more than seventy years. Today there are eighty-five workers in our missions to the Indians.

The story of our first mission field during all these years has been a story of hard slow work, of setbacks and disappointments. Though the missionaries had much to learn, the church that sent them had to learn also. It had to set up principles and rules for its first mission field. The missionaries were pledged to carry out the decisions of their church at home and the church often debated long and hotly about what should be done.

The Christian Reformed Church believes that missionaries are sent to help the native people build up a church of their own. But saying this is not enough, because the church must then decide for every mission post on every field what this means in terms of money and men and schools and hospitals and chapels.

And so there are sad pages in the story of our mission fields, the first one among the Indians and the others which have come since that time in other parts of the world. Sometimes missionaries disagree, as Paul and Barnabas did before one of their missionary trips. Sometimes it is the church at home that is not as helpful as it could be, making the missionaries' work difficult.

But the story of our Indian mission field is not only one of hard work and special problems. It is also a story of faithfulness, of God's faithfulness despite our stumbling. It is a story of the faithfulness and patience of many missionaries, some of whom have given twenty, thirty, up to forty-five years of their lives working among the Navajo and Zuni Indians. It is a story of joy, too, because through the Christian Reformed Church Christ is gathering many souls for his kingdom from the Indian reservations of the wide southwest.

THE LORD MADE ROOM

When Isaac had his herdsmen dig new wells for him, there was one place he called Rehoboth. "For now the Lord has made room for us," he said.

The Christian Reformed Church also needed room for its work on the Indian field. When the Lord opened the way to a place of three hundred acres just off the reservation, we called it Rehoboth after the place of Isaac's day. In our Rehoboth too there was need for a well. The first attempts to drill one in this dry land did not succeed. Finally in 1929 a driller was hired at great cost to drill sixteen hundred feet into the earth. One day he telephoned excitedly to Business Manager Bosscher who was away at a Bible conference. "We've struck an artesian flow," he said, "and the water is running a quarter of a mile down the flat." God had answered much prayer and sent a great supply of good water that still flows freely today.

The three hundred acres of Smith's Ranch had only a few frame buildings when we bought it in 1902 for sixteen hundred dollars. Today Rehoboth is a whole little Christian Reformed town. On its tree-lined streets stand a church, a hospital, grade school and high school, dormitories, industrial buildings, homes, post office, and more.

Rehoboth is the center of our work with the Navajos. Sixty Indian boys and sixty Indian girls sleep in the dormitories of the schools. There is a waiting list of other children who would like to come. A doctor and his staff are in charge of the hospital with its thirty beds and ten little cribs in the nursery. Many Indians come to the clinics every day. The Rehoboth church is an organized church and its minister also works among the hospital patients.

Other names have become dear to us on the Indian field, names of mission posts opened as more missionaries came to serve. They lie up in the northwest part of New Mexico, many of them not far from the Arizona border. The Navajo reservation stretches into both states, but we have agreed to work in New Mexico while the Presbyterian church agreed to work on that part of the reservation in Arizona.

Tohatchi is the oldest of these Navajo posts. Its name means Little Water, a true name for many years when the water trickled slowly from the hillside and the Indian school children dipped it up in a tin cup. Mr. Vander Wagen did not forget his first trip to Tohatchi two years after he came to the southwest. He was lost on the way, had to send his Indian guide back for fresh horses, and tipped over in an arroyo during the black of night, landing on the ground with all the supplies on top of him.

Two Grey Hills was another of our early Navajo posts. It takes its name from two wide grey hills that stand out on the plain. Here we bought mission buildings from the Baptists, but a windstorm took away the missionary's home. The new post was built nearby at Toadlena, meaning Flowing Water, after a stream that flows there.

Over in the east of the reservation lies Crown Point, in a valley with pointed hills around that look like the points of a crown. Some called it the crown of all our stations because God blessed the work here abundantly, especially through Missionary and Mrs. J. R. Bolt who worked in Crown Point for twenty-five years. From Crown Point began the mission at San Antone, standing on a hill near the entrance to a canyon.

No one in Navajoland forgot the winter of 1931, the winter of the big snow. Especially the new missionary at Two Wells remembered it, for he had just arrived there. Two days later there were ninety-four Indians in his basement, caught by the snowstorm while they were picking pinion nuts. Some Indians and many animals froze to death as the snow drifted higher and higher. Army planes dropped food at Two Wells, and it took many weeks for spring to arrive after winter had dropped a hundred twenty inches of snow.

In Gallup, grown large and important as the seat of McKinley County, we have a whitewashed chapel. Several hundred Indian students attend it, and so do other Indians who work or trade in Gallup. Bethany All Tribes Chapel is a gift of the Bethany church in Muskegon and it is there to serve all tribes, as does the busy city in which it stands.

There is Farmington, in fertile country nearer the border of Colorado, and Shiprock, named for a strange red granite rock shaped like a sailing ship. The Indians have a legend that says they arrived on that ship many moons ago. At Red Rock, another post, and at Nahaschitty, north of Toadlena, we have trained Indian workers in charge. All over the field there are Indians working with our white missionaries. Some have studied at Calvin College or the Reformed Bible Institute in Grand Rapids.

There are still a dozen missionaries to the Indians whom we have not talked about. They work on the little reservation of the Zuni tribe. Sometimes we forget how different the Zunis and the Navajos are. Their languages are as different as Chinese and English. The Zuni is a farmer while the Navajo is a herdsman. The Zuni tribe numbers only three thousand and all these tribespeople live in one square mile. Instead of hogans widely scattered, the Zunis live close together, in a series of adobe homes called their pueblo. Just as tightly as their homes are built together, so tightly the Zuni people also cling together. Everyone stays in the group, locked in by many fears of the gods and the evil spirits, the white man and anything new.

Andrew Vander Wagen was our first missionary in Zuni when we took over that field after the Presbyterians had left it. "Van" came to the rows of flat mud houses attached together, some on top of others. He saw the twisting streets of Zuni village and the ladders of poles and sticks up which the families climbed to their homes on the second and third stories. He saw their flat-topped holy mountain nearby and he knew how the Zunis hated the white missionary, how they had even killed the priests of Rome who came long before.

Missionary Vander Wagen offered to help the Zunis with their farming and introduced his wife as a nurse. Strangely, the Zunis welcomed him. The headman and the chief highpriest stood before him and Naochi, the chief warrior, said, "Your words have not only entered into our ears, but have lodged in our hearts."

When smallpox struck the pueblo, it was Van and his wife who worked night and day. He also gathered Zuni words with an interpreter named Tumaka, and he bought the mission property for a hundred dollars. On this land, just across the Zuni riverbed from the main village, the chapel and the day school were begun. Today a principal and six teachers give Zuni children Christian training there.

Changes are taking place in Zuni village, the largest Indian village in the world. Though its people are locked together in their fears, they are seeing how the love of God can take fear away from the Christians. The Zuni families and young people who stand for Christ have had to stand alone, hated by the rest of the tribe. But through their faithful lives, even more than through the white missionaries, the Zuni people begin to see what Christ can mean to them.

A new generation is growing up among the Indians. The young people of this generation go to schools and take jobs and understand the white man's world better than their grandparents did.

153

Some are already Christians because their parents turned to Christ. Others are more ready than before to hear from the white missionary about the true God.

We spend time especially with this new generation, even sending missionaries to their schools off the reservation, because we hope that the new leaders of the Navajos and Zunis can be won for the Lord. If they are, the Gospel of Christ will have a fuller place in the hogan and the pueblo and wherever the Indian finds his new place.

THE BIG MISSIONARY

The Navajos called him *Dineh Bikis*, The Big Missionary. When they saw his team of white horses coming in the distance, they hurried to make ready for him. He sat with them around their campfires, talking their language, eating their roasted mutton, drinking their coffee. While he stayed, before he drove his horses on to other hogans, the big missionary spoke to his Indian friends about the great true God and his son Jesus.

All his life Leonard Peter Brink planned to come to the Indians. When he was a small boy his father told him Indian stories at the fireside of their home in what is now Saugatuck, Michigan. Sometimes real Indians passed up and down the rivers nearby. The Indians of our land do not know of God and the Bible, said father Brink to his first son. Someone must tell them.

Leonard thought of his father's words. One day he set up a row of kitchen chairs and preached a sermon to the Indians he pretended were sitting there.

When he came to New Mexico from western Michigan, Leonard Brink was a man, graduated from the seminary. There he had been given the nickname that stayed with him all his life. "L.P." his classmates called him, to keep him apart from another student named Brink. Everywhere in the church and on the Indian field people knew L.P. by those two initials. All his articles and letters he signed that way.

When L.P. came to the Indians of the Navajo reservation, he came to stay. For thirty-five years he lived and worked among them. His body rests with them today.

It was the year 1900, when New Mexico was not yet a state, that L.P. and his wife got off the Sante Fe train and stood among the bars and saloons of Gallup. The first missionaries welcomed them, and the next morning the Brinks set out for their new post in a wagon drawn by a team of horses, one wild and the other crippled. Over the twisting trail, through dry arroyos and across

155

a wide plain, L.P. brought his wife to Tohatchi, at the foot of a mountain. Here they found their home, its mud walls cracked and crooked, its old cook stove propped up on bricks.

To get supplies they had to go the twenty-five miles to Gallup. Each time it took them two days. At night they slept out under the stars on hay which they fed to the horses the next morning. When the howl of coyotes came too near, L.P. fired a shot from his revolver to frighten them, and then went back to sleep until the howls came near again.

In his own eyes L.P. was not the big missionary. It is all God's sovereign grace in me, he said, and went on working as hard as ever.

Yet this missionary does have a special place among all the faithful missionaries of our Indian field. God did give him a bigness, not only in the way he looked, but in what he thought and in what he did.

He traveled all over the reservation and he knew it well. His mind was full of plans for spreading the Lord's work. L.P. looked so far ahead that some of his hopes are just now beginning to come true. New mission posts, training schools for Indian workers, Indian churches forming a classis of their own — all these were in his mind. He looked in faith, not doubting that the Lord could bring it to pass.

L.P. did not only think and plan. He worked. Even when his body began to break down under the strain of being so busy in a high altitude, he did not slow his pace. Besides taking care of his own mission post, he was a leader on the whole field.

It was he who first learned the difficult Navajo language well enough to translate into it. His is the honor of giving the Navajos many parts of the Bible in their own tongue. *God Bi-zad,* God's

Word, is the name on the cover of the first of these translations published as a book by the American Bible Society.

L.P. translated more — the forms for marriage and the Lord's Supper and baptism, a catechism book, a hymnbook. He made it possible for a new kind of music to be heard in Navajoland. In their own tongue, the Indians were singing the songs of the church, a sweeter stronger music than the weird wild melodies of the pagan festivals.

If the Indian learned from L.P., so did the white people of the Christian Reformed Church which sent him. Endless articles appeared signed with his initials. Later he started a special magazine, *The Christian Indian,* of which he was editor. He wrote poems and songs in both Dutch and English. Often at the end of a year we sing his translation in our Psalter Hymnal, "Hours and days and years and ages swift as moving shadows flee . . . "

The big missionary is buried among the Indians whom he loved and who loved him. By his life among them he had become a part of their history, and some of them had become a part of the kingdom of heaven.

BEFORE THE BAMBOO CURTAIN

While the doors of China were open to friends from other lands, the Christian Reformed Church had a mission there. It was our first mission in a foreign country.

There had been some talk of sending missionaries to Egypt or Persia, to Cuba or the Dutch islands of Bali and New Guinea. But these ideas gave way to greater talk about China or Central Africa, where Johanna Veenstra of our church had just begun to work under the Sudan United Mission.

A committee studied the problem for a year and spoke in favor of Africa. But the synod of 1920 thought otherwise. We will send two men to make a beginning in China, they said. China is an important country with a healthful climate, and its people are more like us than the Africans are.

The Christian Reformed Mission to China lasted almost thirty years. Its headquarters were in the old walled city of Jukao, not far from the coast and about fifty miles north of Shanghai and the important Yangtze River. Jukao's wall was wide and went all around the city, with four gates guarded by old cannon. There was also a canal running all around the city outside the wall. Four bridges crossed the canal, which was part of a whole network of canals, the water highways connecting the towns and cities of the province.

After the first three missionaries went out, more were sent. For a time there were twelve of them with their families. Along the narrow streets of Jukao the Christian Reformed Church established chapels, a hospital, and a home for our doctor. Outside the east gate and over the east gate bridge were built the other missionary homes and a Christian school for missionary children.

The work spread to fifteen neighboring towns. Native workers and evangelists helped the missionaries. The Chinese long had been serving a strange mixture of three religions, following the man Confucius, the idol Buddha, and the superstitions of Taoism. Some now left these behind and were baptized into the name of the Father and the Son and the Holy Spirit. They learned to leave behind their shrines and temples and sacrificing to their ancestors.

But the Chinese are both polite and crafty people. Often they seemed to the missionary to be very interested in his message when they really were not. And so the work in China also had its unexpected disappointments.

Three wars struck China during the life of our mission there. Usually the missionaries had to leave their posts. Sometimes they stayed, facing danger and death. When the Japanese attacked the city of Jukao in 1938, two of our missionaries were there. They opened the compound outside the city to care for a thousand refugee women and children who stayed for many weeks.

After each war the missionaries returned to build up the Chinese churches again. But there came a time of no return. A new god had come to China under a red flag. He would have no god but himself. With an iron hand, he pulled down the bamboo curtain and fastened it, shutting in half a billion people to be his slaves, and shutting out the Christian world whose missionaries had brought the true God.

And so in 1950 our work in China came to a stop. Today we can only wonder what has happened to the mission buildings and the Chinese Christians behind the tightly drawn curtain.

There is one thing we can do. We pray for all Christians of China, that their faith fail not under the iron hand that is upon them.

"BUT I PRESS ON"

Behind the bamboo curtain there is a grave that the Christian Reformed Church does not forget. It is in the white man's cemetery on Bubbling Well Road in Shanghai, and it holds the body of a medical missionary of whom someone said, He was too big for us.

Lee S. Huizenga was indeed a giant in his accomplishments. He was a minister, loved for his preaching and his leadership. He was a doctor twice over, once in medicine and again in public health. He was an author of books and articles, many of which he wrote while traveling on shipboard, because he had no other time for writing. He became world famous for his knowledge of leprosy, and he was sent with authority to many places. Among his friends he numbered ambassadors and scientists, scholars and men of wealth, and he received honors at home and abroad.

But none of this mattered much to Dr. Huizenga. He was dedicated to a greater work, and he never rested from it. "I count not myself to have apprehended. . . But I press on," he said over and over in the words of Paul. Hard he leaned on the Lord to show him the way and to give him the strength. With this leading and this power, and with a devoted wife to help him, Lee Huizenga lived a full brilliant life of preaching and healing and writing. An adventure in faith, his best friend called it.

Often he moved alone, not appreciated by the people of his own Christian Reformed churches. His mind and his faith were too big for many of them to understand. They did not see until much later that through his amazing work they had made a gift to the world, to the larger church of Christ on earth. It was a great gift, long remembered.

160

Mother Huizenga said about her youngest son Lee that he was a child "asked of the Lord for the Lord." From the time he drove his father's few cows to the meadow, and during the time he worked in a print shop to earn money for college, Lee Huizenga's eyes were turned to foreign lands. He saw himself standing there somewhere, preaching in another language to people who needed Christ. To help them still more, he decided to become a doctor as well as a minister.

For many years Dr. Huizenga dreamed of South America. But God did not open that door to him. Waiting, he went to work among the Indians of our mission field in the southwest. There his writing began. "This experience among the Indians made me dip my pen into the ink for the first time," he said later, "and it has never been dry since."

But while he traveled on horseback from hogan to hogan, his eyes still looked for an open door across an ocean. There was a time when it seemed to be Africa and he was eager to go there. Instead God turned him around and opened another door. Through it Lee Huizenga went confidently to twenty-five years of missionary work in China.

He was one of our first three men in that new field, and he opened our mission hospital in Jukao. In a two-wheeled cart pulled by a Chinese servant he went to the homes of those who called for him. As a doctor he healed their bodies and as a minister he told them of healing for their souls.

Dr. Huizenga became interested in tuberculosis and especially in leprosy, knowing that half the lepers of the world were in China. He treated hundreds of them in his own clinics, and he became an expert on leprosy, studying and speaking and writing about it. The United States sent him as its delegate to a leprosy conference in Cairo, Egypt. He was loaned by our church for a six months inspection tour of all the leper colonies in the Pacific.

While the wars stopped the work of many missionaries, they only increased the work of Dr. Huizenga. In Shanghai he was asked to take charge of hospitals, of leper and tuberculosis hospitals as well as regular hospitals. He started an orphanage. He made radio broadcasts and preached. He worked with Jewish refugees who had fled from Hitler's persecutions in Europe. He was well known to the Chinese government, and he passed out medical supplies from America to the places that needed them most.

The days were never long enough. He and his family lived in a few small rooms and had to move often. The Huizengas were in

162

Shanghai when the Japanese took the city, when the streets were crowded with homeless starving refugees, when fires and dead bodies lay in their way as they went to their work at the leper hospitals.

Thousands of other missionaries had left China in time. But the Lord had given Dr. Huizenga endless work to do, and he took this as a sign that he should not leave it for the safety of America. Once he had written, "I just want to be so filled with the blessed Spirit of God that I can show the world that I am not of the world, yet in the world for the world." And so he stayed in the strange war-torn land that had become a second home to him, and he went on working with people of other churches and other lands at a time when they needed him desperately.

At first he worked freely. But the last two years of his life Lee Huizenga and his family were war prisoners of the Japanese in a Shanghai concentration camp called Chapei. The order to enter it came in April of 1943. Though the American doctor was their prisoner, the Japanese respected him and put him in charge of all the medical work in the camp. It was hard work, with few supplies to use and meager food to live on. But the Lord was making ready to release the prisoner who had pressed on for years, making every minute count.

Lee Huizenga had written of his death. A few years before it came, he said, "I have stepped ashore in many harbors, ever with the feeling that I was a stranger after all. But when we finally weigh anchor here and arrive beyond, at once we'll be at home with the Lord."

He entered that last harbor one stormy summer midnight. While the sound of thunder and of bombs shook the city of Shanghai, he left it behind. The adventure in faith was finished. The Lord called him to come home.

BLACK DIAMONDS

There was once a brave white woman who went alone to Africa in search of black diamonds. She wanted them for the crown of a king, the king who made the heavens and the earth. Perhaps she was thinking of the song about precious jewels when she spoke of the black diamonds, because the treasure she came seeking in the jungle land of Nigeria was the treasure of black men's souls for the king of all kings.

In the country of Nigeria on Africa's west coast flows the large river Niger, which empties into the ocean and which gives the land its name. Into the Niger flows another long river called the Benue. It was up the grey-green waters of the Benue that a flat-bottomed river barge carried the white woman the last three hundred miles of her journey. Twelve black men poled the small boat along, and it took two weeks of traveling under the scorching sun of the dry season before the barge came to the mission station called Ibi.

Probably no white woman had ever made such a river trip alone before, and the black men watched her curiously. She watched them, too, understanding nothing of what they said. The first evening the men had an argument, and one pulled out a long knife. In her fear that they were deciding whether to kill her and steal her baggage, the lone passenger remembered the motto she had chosen for her life. "Be strong and of a good courage," it reminded her in the words of God to Joshua. "Be not afraid, neither be thou dismayed, for the Lord is with thee whithersoever thou goest."

These words lingered in the heart of the white woman as she set up her folding cot in the boat on the river that first night, while

her black crew stretched out around their campfire on a sandbar. Through the darkness there came the strange calls and night sounds of the jungle. But God had said "whithersoever thou goest," and this was promise enough for the white woman. Exhausted with the heat and new experiences of the day, she fell asleep.

Thirteen years later, as the dawn light came into the sky on a Palm Sunday morning, Johanna Veenstra went to stand before the king for whom she had come to Africa. He called her unexpectedly, before she was forty years old, and when her work was beginning to bear much fruit. After saving her from poisonous snakes and jungle climate illnesses, God took her from the green-roofed mission hospital at Vom, high on a plateau, where she had undergone a seemingly successful operation for appendicitis.

In the quiet of the little cemetery where Miss Veenstra was the first white person to be laid, friends both black and white stood at the open grave. They sang a hymn in the Hausa language and bowed their heads for a Hausa prayer. Then they walked slowly the half mile back to the hospital, talking as they went about all that Johanna Veenstra had begun to do from the mission station at Lupwe.

On the grave now stands a simple cement cross, behind which a cactus plant stretches out its long green spears. Beneath the name on the flat stone there are the glorious words of Paul which were true also of the life of the white woman buried there, "For me to live is Christ."

SEE WHAT GOD HAS DONE

Today the Christian Reformed Church thanks God for the woman who inspired our church at home to take over the work she had been doing at the mission station Lupwe.

Lupwe was a new station four miles from the village of the big chief at Takum. It was only a few unfinished huts when Miss Veenstra's native carriers set down the sixty-pound loads they had carried on their heads more than fifty miles by jungle trails. The dishes stood on the dirt floor at first and clothes lay over a rope

166

stretched from one side of the hut to the other. But there was a spring of fresh water at Lupwe, and water is important in Africa. More than this, there was peace in the wide green plain around Lupwe. Here the pagan wickednesses of the native villages could not bother those whom Miss Veenstra hoped would come to the mission school.

Soon six hospital huts were built, one for medicines and examining, the others for patients too sick to go home. They were cared for by members of their families who came along to stay with them.

From Lupwe Miss Veenstra went on hard treks through her district, bicycling along bumpy trails, walking and climbing where the bicycle could not go. In many tucked-away villages where no white person had been seen before, she spoke in the Hausa language about the great God who made the world and sent his son to die for those who believe on him.

There were several black diamonds that stood out in the early story of Lupwe. One was Nasamu, an orphan whom a big chief made his slave. Many times Nasamu begged the chief to let him go to the mission school and finally he said, "Even if you cut my body in pieces, I must go to school and learn about the Book and about God." So the chief consented. Nasamu learned and believed, and when he was baptized he took the Christian name Daniel.

Filibbus, from the important town of Wukari, was another first believer. He studied on, and became the first teacher in the mission school at Lupwe. And then there was Istifanus, who prayed eight years for his wife before she too became a Christian. These men were the first elders in the Lupwe-Takum area. Istifanus, who lived longer than the other two, became our first full native minister and he has been working faithfully for the Lord more than twenty-five years.

On her furloughs in the United States, Johanna Veenstra spoke of her work and persuaded two Christian Reformed teachers to join her. Today these women are the veteran missionaries of our African field. One is Miss Jennie Stielstra and the other is Mrs. Edgar Smith, whose husband was with the British missions in Nigeria until he married her and came to work in the Lupwe district. Today he is a minister of the Christian Reformed Church.

Seven years after Miss Veenstra's death, what she had often hoped and prayed for came true. In 1940 the Christian Reformed Church officially took over her work in the Lupwe area, and our church then became a member of the Sudan United Mission, under whom Miss Veenstra had worked.

The Sudan United Mission, or the S.U.M. as it is often called, is made up of churches from different countries who want to see the true Gospel preached in Africa. It began in England with a group of men who dreamed of the day when a chain of Christian churches would stretch all across the dark continent. Fifty years after the S.U.M. had built its first mission house from red clay bricks near the Wase Rock, the mission could report to the governor of northern Nigeria that in two thousand places of his territory a quarter of a million people gathered each Sunday to worship the one true God. The governor was surprised. He could hardly believe that Christianity had moved so fast among his people.

The S.U.M. in Nigeria is divided into five regions. One of these regions is the work of a Danish church and two are of American churches, one of these the Christian Reformed Church. The others are sponsored by Missionary Societies in England and South Africa. The regions co-operate in things that matter to all of them. With a sixth independent mission, the S.U.M. missions have asked to be incorporated as a fellowship of African churches, called the Tarayar Ekklesiyoyin Kristi A Sudan.

In the Hausa district where Johanna Veenstra began her work at Lupwe, and in the new large Tiv area which we have promised gradually to take over, the Christian Reformed Church has more than thirty white missionary workers in the churches, hospitals, and schools. But they are not enough, because the work in Africa is big and calling to be done. Who of us — ministers, teachers, doctors, nurses — who of us will go?

TELLING AND PRAYING AND GIVING

One of the large green hills that stand around the Lupwe plain has been named Mount Veenstra. From it can be seen the grass roofs and the newer shining aluminum roofs of the buildings on the Lupwe compound. In the evening there is the glow of electric lights amid the darkness all around.

Every day the waiting room at the hospital is full of people seeking help with malaria, snake bite, sleeping sickness, a skin disease called yaws, and pneumonia which comes when the cold winds strike brown bodies only thinly clothed. There are classes meeting, often outside, the classes of the primary school, and the special classes for evangelists and pastors taught by the Reverend and Mrs. Smith. We have more than forty native evangelists, each responsible for the teaching and preaching in a village or small area. Some evangelists are receiving still more training and may in time become full pastors as Istifanus is. We are also working with the S.U.M. to set up a special school for native pastors.

From Lupwe the road goes around one side of Mount Veenstra to the town of Takum with six thousand people in it. Here Istifanus is the pastor, and though he is past sixty, he still goes many miles each month on his bicycle to bring the sacraments to churches where the evangelists may not perform them because they are not ordained pastors.

Around Mount Veenstra to the other side is the colony of leper patients who have come to Lupwe to stay for treatment. There are six hundred of them living in huts they have made themselves, and they grow their own food. Twice a week they take the sulphone tablets which have made such a difference in the treatment of leprosy. Three times a year a doctor comes to see by tests who is cured and ready to go home. But leprosy is a long disease and only about sixty patients out of the six hundred go home each year. Meanwhile they learn about Christ and worship in their own church at the foot of the hill. Those who do go home often take with them not only cured bodies but also a changed heart.

Fifty-six miles through the jungle is Baissa, a town of two hundred people, where a white minister, teacher, and nurse make their headquarters for work with the dozens of little villages in the rows of green hills beyond. The minister is often trekking and he can tell many stories of escape from poisonous snakes, rising rivers, and illnesses. In Wukari, the largest town of the district with eight thousand people, we have a third white missionary station. Here too there is the teaching and the preaching.

The work of the Christian Reformed Church in Nigeria is in the wide middle belt of the country. For the first ten years we were in the area around Lupwe which we call the Hausa district because the fifteen small tribes who live here have learned the Hausa language in addition to the languages of their own tribes. So the Hausa language is a kind of trade language which most of the people understand and which our missionaries learn and use in their work.

Next to the Hausa district is a very large area called the Tiv district. While the Hausa tribes are only three to six thousand people each, the Tiv tribe is huge and the people who speak the Tiv language number eight hundred thousand. The Tiv country is more open and civilized than the jungle land of the Hausa district. Trees have been cut down, and wild animals are few though monkeys and snakes are everywhere in Africa. The Tiv people are farmers, too, but they live in little groups of two or three houses rather than in villages.

For many years the Dutch Reformed Church of South Africa worked in the Tiv district, setting up schools and hospitals and establishing churches. But the South African church was also

171

working among the Basuto people in South Africa. This work greatly increased, and so it was agreed that the Christian Reformed Church would gradually take over the Tiv work in addition to the Hausa work.

This was a big promise, bigger than most of us at home could realize. First there was the Tiv land east of the broad Katsina Ala River. When this and the Hausa district were counted together, the area still to be ours west of the river was three or four times as big. We have just begun to work in the first place across the river.

In the places already under our church in the Tiv and Hausa districts, there are about ten thousand people in church every Sunday morning. The secret of this number and of the growth of our African church is worth knowing and copying here at home.

The secret does not lie in the preaching of the few white missionaries, but in the telling which each new Christian does. He talks to his family and his neighbors about the good news. He gets them together in his hut and with charcoal he writes on the walls what little he has learned about reading the Bible. One to another the gospel goes on its way, with every native believer a working witness for the Lord.

The people of our churches in Africa are praying people. At sunrise every morning the sound of bells brings them to church for prayers. Often the bell is only a piece of railroad track tied on a pole and hit with another piece of metal track. The evangelist leads the prayers and others take part. So each day begins with a prayer meeting.

The African church is also a giving church. Its people pay for their own churches, schools, evangelists, and teachers. Twice a year they bring an extra tithe of their crops which are sold and the money added to the church treasury. Of all that comes in, ten

172

per cent goes for missions among their own people, and evangelists are paid to go to new villages to preach. In this way the Baissa church began because the Takum church sent three evangelists to work there.

This telling, praying, giving church in Nigeria is part of the Africa which is waking up and catching up to the rest of the world. The native people want to learn and do for themselves. And so the white missionaries work to help the church learn and do for itself, too, so that it may be a leader and a blessing in the new Africa. It will be a long time before the guiding and teaching of the white missionary is no longer needed. In these important years we of the Christian Reformed Church have a great challenge as the church of God's black diamonds moves onward behind the cross of Jesus.

Sometimes the school boys sing that song, Onward Christian Soldiers, as they march to church on Sunday morning in Lupwe. Down the brown path they come, dressed in white, barefoot, single file and in step, singing in music we all know the Hausa words they best know:

> *Yakin Almasihu, Yanuwa mu ke yi;*
> *Gabanmu ya tafi, binsa mu ke yi.*

BROTHERS IN NEED

How do we decide where to send missionaries? How does Christ show us the places we should go to speak for him?

We went to the American Indian because he was in our own country, not knowing Christ. We chose the land of China to set up our first mission abroad. In Africa we entered the field where Johanna Veenstra had begun her work. Today we have a missionary-teacher in Formosa, too. And there are other countries—Ethiopia, Pakistan, India—where members of the Christian Reformed Church work as missionary doctors and nurses even though our church does not have a mission there.

There are still other places to which God has led our church and opened the way. To these we have gone because brothers called to us to come over and help them. Some were brothers by blood, Dutch blood, and so we felt a tie to them. All were brothers in the faith, in the Reformed faith as it came through John Calvin and spread around the world.

We cannot defend the faith alone, said these brothers. We lack ministers trained in schools of the Reformed tradition. Can you send such men from among you to strengthen us and teach us?

We will send them, said the Christian Reformed Church in America. We will also open the doors of our college and seminary to men among you. Let them study with us and return to make your church of the Reformed faith stronger.

First it was South America. Later came the calls from Ceylon and Japan, from Australia and New Zealand. To the churches of the Reformed faith in these parts of the world, the Christian Reformed Church, blessed by God, has begun to be a blessing.

174

BETWEEN THE RICH AND THE POOR

Within the sight of gleaming skyscraper cities and gorgeous country estates, a poor man's ox drags a tree over a dirt road to an old sawmill and women work at making bricks from clay with their hands. This is South America, continent of contrasts. Here the

175

rich are very rich, the poor are very poor, and the middle class of people is hard to find. Here the church of Rome has been speaking for centuries in a powerful voice.

Even earlier, as early as the Pilgrims landed on Plymouth Rock, the Dutch were in Brazil as conquerors. In 1636 there was a whole classis of Dutch Reformed churches on the eastern coast. But the Dutch sold their rights to Portugal and left. Today the religion and the language of Brazil come from Portugal, just as Spain has left its language and Roman religion in Argentina.

Shortly before 1900 a few thousand Dutch people came to Argentina. This time they came as settlers, not as conquerors. Argentina had made bright promises which she could not keep. Some of the Dutch were sent inland in freight cars. Some died. A devoted Dutch minister gathered those who were left into churches, one church in the important city of Buenos Aires, another in Tres Arroyos, which is the Spanish for "three rivers." Then the minister turned to the stronger church of settlers in North America and asked them to help their brothers in the south.

Later came the colonies of Dutch dairy farmers who settled together in Brazil. They soon set up their cooperatives for milk and for making cheese. The Brazilian government was pleased to have such hard-working settlers among its people. It encouraged more of them to come. The Dutch farmers built their churches and their Christian schools. But they needed leaders. Carembehy, the oldest colony, had to get along many years without a minister of its own.

At first we helped the South American churches with money. Later we sent ministers, two of whom are veterans of twenty years, the Reverend William Muller in Brazil and the Reverend Jerry Pott in Argentina. The first student from a South American church finished his study at Calvin Seminary in 1954 and returned to serve his own people far to the south in Argentina.

In 1956 there were six organized churches in Brazil and Argentina. They call themselves Classis Buenos Aires and · are still counted part of the faraway mother church in the Netherlands. It is an unusual classis, with its Dutch and Spanish and Portuguese languages. When it meets once in three years, some delegates travel more than two thousand miles to attend.

Some day the Reformed churches of South America hope to stand alone, stronger and larger than they are now. As their Dutch language wall comes down, they hope to work with their Spanish-speaking and Portuguese-speaking countrymen. Meanwhile, until that day, we of the Christian Reformed Church in North America count it a privilege to help them.

ISLAND OUTPOST

Around the world, on the little pear-shaped island of Ceylon, we are helping brothers, too. Ceylon lies off the southeast coast of India and it is little bigger than our state of West Virginia. It has a long history of grand civilizations dating back more than a thousand years before Christ.

Soon after Columbus discovered America, the Portuguese established trade with the Sinhalese natives of Ceylon and took control of the island which was rich in ivory and other treasures of the Far East.

Next came the Dutch, who fought twenty years to take Ceylon from Portugal. The Dutch East India Company came with soldiers who conquered the few important towns one by one. They set the Dutch flag flying over the island for one hundred fifty years. Ministers of the Reformed Church in the Netherlands came with the soldiers and stayed to serve the Dutch people who moved in to set up large plantations. This growing number of ministers began to do mission work among the natives, many of whom were Buddhists. In fact, the followers of Buddha believe he ascended into heaven from the top of a cone-shaped mountain in Ceylon where they point to a giant footprint to prove their claim.

The Dutch Reformed Church of Ceylon, begun in 1642, grew rapidly while the Dutch were in power. It came to include two hundred thousand families, more than four times as many families as we have in our Christian Reformed Church today. The Ceylon church supported eighty Christian schools and a large seminary.

In 1795 the British took Ceylon from the Dutch while the Netherlands was at war with France. In the bitter feeling that followed, the Dutch ministers all fled to the Dutch East Indies city of Batavia. This left the large church of Ceylon without any pastors. Many of its families turned to the Church of England which the British brought with them. Some drifted to the Roman church and others went back to pagan Buddhism.

A faithful few clung to their Reformed faith and looked out into the rest of the world to find another Reformed church that would help them. At first the Presbyterians of Scotland, also Calvinists, came to their rescue. Later the Dutch Reformed Church of South Africa helped for a time.

After this the group in Ceylon appealed to Dr. Henry Beets and asked whether his church in America would send ministers to help. We want to keep the faith of our fathers, they said, but the spirit of forsaking it is creeping in among us. We are losing our hold.

It took time to send help, as all things seem to take time in the careful Christian Reformed Church. Finally in 1949 the first Christian Reformed minister, the Reverend John O. Schuring,

178

went to Ceylon with his family. In the modern capital city of Colombo, among the seven Dutch Reformed churches there, he began to preach and to build up. Soon two other ministers joined him and synod agreed to send two more. Meanwhile, Ceylonese students arrived to study in our college and seminary.

To this interesting outpost of the Reformed faith, on an island of rice and coconut growers, of tea and rubber plantations, of jungle and elephants, the Christian Reformed Church has sent men to help especially in the capital city. Perhaps the Lord will be pleased to use this help to raise up a sturdy pure church among our brothers and to make it a voice for him in the troubled southeast of Asia.

AMONG THE TEMPLES AND THE TORII

The land of the rising sun has many millions of people crowded together on its string of Pacific islands. These Japanese are the most educated people in the world, and they are always reading. They love beautiful things. Almost every family has a little formal garden as a real part of its home. They are people who have a special art of arranging flowers, who make a lovely ceremony out of drinking tea. In their homes with light sliding walls, they glide quietly around, leaving their *geta,* their wooden sandals, outside.

The Japanese worship a strange mixture of religions. Some of it is worship of the idol god Buddha, whose temples and images stand everywhere. Some of it is worship of the Shinto faith, for centuries the state religion. Shinto shrines are always marked by the *torii,* two tall upright posts holding up two crosspieces. Under the *torii* processions never stop, as people clack along in their *geta,* bringing copper coins and other offerings to the shrines. The Japanese worship people, too. They have shrines for famous em-

179

perors and warriors and other heroes of the past. They worship their ancestors and burn incense to them. There are even special idols and shrines for children, and no Japanese home is complete without its god shelf in the corner.

To these Oriental people of the Far East the newest mission of the Christian Reformed Church came in 1951. The doors of China, long open, had been closed. The doors of Japan suddenly became wide open. God used a war to open them. When we occupied Japan after defeating her in the second world war, General Douglas MacArthur invited Christian missionaries to come. The Japanese were very interested in what made America great. They wanted to know all about our democracy and our way of living and our so-called Christian religion.

There was another invitation from Japan which came especially to our church. It was the call of brothers, brothers with names like Fujii and Matsuo and Tokiwa. During the war the Japanese government had ordered all Christian churches to unite into one church, which was called the Nippon Kiristo Kyodan. When General MacArthur proclaimed religious liberty again, many Christian churches stayed in the Kyodan. But the Kyodan cannot stand for a strong Christian faith because it is a mixture of so many different kinds. It has become cold and formal and not interested in bringing new souls to Christ.

There were a few churches who stepped out of the Kyodan to be by themselves again, to preach and to work as they believed, even though they had to give up the money and help which the Kyodan churches received. One of these brave groups was the little Reformed Church of Japan, with only eight ministers and eight churches when it made its declaration of independence nine months after the war ended in 1945.

"The hope of the world is in the God of Calvinism," said the Reformed Church of Japan. "God, let thy holy work which thou hast already begun within us be completed. Amen."

180

The Reverend Albert Smit, our last missionary out of China, was asked to stop in Japan to talk with these brothers. He reported their need to the church at home, and synod decided to give help. In 1951 the first three missionaries of the Christian Reformed Japan Mission arrived among the seven million people of Tokyo. They bought the first missionary homes and began to study the language.

By the year of our Centennial there were seven missionaries in Japan. Each started his work with two years of language study in Toyko and then moved to a new place where he began to preach and establish a church. When such new churches become established, they are added to the Reformed Church of Japan. Until then they are under the Christian Reformed Japan Mission, which works side by side with the Japanese church, but is separate from it.

Our mission in Japan is in its early years. Some missionaries are still studying in Tokyo. Only a few have gone to work in other places, where each is helped by a trained native evangelist or assistant. The missionaries work in cities, because even the farmers in Japan live together in cities or villages and go each day to their rice paddies in the countryside.

One of our missionaries is the only foreigner living in the lakeside city of Suwa with forty thousand people. Another missionary is in the Kofu area, which lies within a circle of mountains and is well known for the grapes whose vines trail even over the little farmhouse roofs. In Kawagoe the missionary used a square room of his home for a meeting place and spoke to people who squatted before him Japanese-style on *tatami*, straw mats.

In many ways and many places, through preaching and study classes, with sound trucks and street messages, in schools and hospitals and rented meeting rooms, the work of the Christian Reformed Japan Mission grows.

181

Sometimes God points the way to new places unexpectedly. One of our missionaries was stuck in his car on a muddy mountain road. He found a man with a water buffalo to pull him out, but a short distance farther he was forced to stop because a bridge had washed out. It was night and the missionary decided to sleep in his car. When he awoke in the morning, thirty Japanese children were gathered around, peering in curiously at the strange white man. A kind old woman fed him a breakfast of dried minnows, seaweed, raw egg, and cold rice. She listened eagerly to the missionary and offered to hold meetings in her home if he would come back again and tell her neighbors about Jesus. In the months that followed the first convert of that mountain village was baptized, and all because a washed-out bridge stopped a missionary where he did not plan to stop at all.

While the sliding walls of Japanese homes are open to the missionary and his message, we go on working in the land of the rising sun. Glad we are to help build up a church of Reformed brothers, clasping their hands as we clasp the hands of other brothers in the faith around the world.

THE RADIO VOICE

Every week a man goes into a Chicago skyscraper and makes his
way to the midwest headquarters of one of the largest radio net-
works in the world. Here, in a studio reserved for him, he sits at
a table and reads his message for the week into a microphone,
watching for time signals from the engineer who is recording the
words on tape in the control room.

Meanwhile, during the same week, a choir of seventy picked
students gathers in the Calvin College auditorium in Grand Rapids, with their director, a radio announcer, and an engineer. Carefully they record the music and the words which open and close

183

the weekly program. Then the tape of the message and the tape of the music are put together and sent out, so that people from coast to coast can sit at their radios on Sunday and hear the familiar greeting, "This is the Back to God Hour, the radio voice of the Christian Reformed Church."

More than ten years we had been talking about a church radio broadcast before we had one. We could reach many on the air, said men among us. Let us buy radio time and have the faith that God will use it for his good.

The radio voice had a small beginning on one Chicago station in 1939 when it was heard each week for three months. Eight years later and ever since, the Back to God Hour has been a program heard throughout the year on three hundred stations. It is heard in Canada as well as in the United States. In Alaska people hear it, in Panama and in Ecuador. The synod of 1956 decided to make the Back to God Hour heard still farther around the world.

Today our radio voice is not just one more religious program. It is among the best, the most listened to. Imagine almost four million people, twenty times as many people as we have in the whole Christian Reformed Church, sitting each Sunday at their radios to hear the Back to God Hour. What a tremendous listening audience!

It is an audience of all kinds of people. From the letters that pour in, they introduce themselves. We find them rich and poor, sick and well, young and old, well-educated and unable to spell even common words. There are letters from prisoners stamped with the mark of the prison censor, as well as letters from professors and teachers who write on the dignified stationery of their universities and colleges. Men in government — judges, congressmen, a city council president, a lieutenant governor, a secretary of state. Editors and newspapermen, a man in South Africa who translates the messages into the language of his people, a woman in Seattle whose staff translates the sermons into Chinese and sends them to southeast Asia. The letters come from priests and rabbis, Mormons and Quakers, followers of the new cults, and sincere Christians of every kind of church. Ministers, many of them, ask for sermons and booklets to give to their people. It would be hard to name the kind of person who has not written to the Back to God Hour.

The radio network itself respects the program highly. When it decided to do a special New Year's broadcast one year, it chose our radio minister and choir to do it, though it had many other religious programs from which to choose.

The Back to God Hour has had a full-time minister for more than ten years. He is the Reverend Peter Eldersveld, a man whom God has blessed with special talents for this special work of speaking to the world around us.

The broadcast has a home, too, in a two-story brick and white stone office building. Here on the first floor behind large glass block windows, eleven staff members of the Back to God Hour work, planning, writing, producing, and mailing.

The mailing is a large job because through the years the Back to God Hour has done more for its listeners than broadcast to them. It sends reading material into their homes. Every week forty thousand copies of the Sunday message roll off the presses and are sent to those who ask for them. There is other literature for the asking or at a small cost —-lessons in Bible study, book lists for Christian reading, copies of the creeds of our church and clear explanations of our doctrines.

Especially there is a little monthly booklet called *The Family Altar*, which has helped thousands of families to have their family worship together each day. For each day of the month there is Scripture reading, a short meditation, and a prayer. Almost eighty-five thousand *Family Altars* are mailed out every month, most of them to families outside the Christian Reformed Church.

Some go to hospitals, missions, and prisons. In Ceylon our missionaries use a thousand of them each month. In Illinois a Catholic chaplain in a Veterans' Hospital brings two hundred fifty around to his sick men. One church places copies in all the motels of their area. Four hundred *Family Altars* go monthly to the State Penitentiary of Louisiana. No one can tell how many broken down family altars have been repaired, how many new family altars have been built through this service of the Back to God Hour.

Our church began to speak by radio because we want to share what we believe with the people of America. We want them to know how the Word of God, explained in the Reformed faith after the way of John Calvin, can help them in every part of their living.

The Back to God Hour speaks this message in a clear, up-to-date way. Its words have dignity, not shouting, and its music is found in the hymns and anthems of Christ's church. To the surprise of those who doubted, our radio voice has been the answer for many hungry hearts.

Sometimes the people of our churches do not stand behind the radio voice as well as they could. Listeners to our broadcast have come eagerly to our churches, and found some of us unfriendly or uninterested in them.

But slowly we are learning. As the wall comes down and we stand among our American neighbors, we find what the Back to God Hour has been finding for years—that we have a faith and a church these neighbors need and want, if we will only bring them into it with love, and patiently.

THE NEW FRONTIER

When Jesus told his disciples to be his witnesses he said, Begin at home, in Jerusalem where you are living. Christ also speaks those words to us who are his witnesses today. Begin to speak for me at home, he says. Tell your neighbors the good news and share my earthly church with them. This witnessing at home is the church's work of home missions.

In the Christian Reformed Church another kind of work has also been called home missions. It is the work of gathering into churches in new places people who already believe in Christ. For many years we have been very busy setting up these churches all over the United States and Canada. Wherever a group of Dutch-Americans settled and wanted to become part of our church, we have sent home missionaries and spent money to help.

In the earliest years, the regular ministers went around helping to begin these new churches, besides taking care of their own. But they could not do it all. The first full-time home missionary was a Christian school teacher who answered the church's call for "a traveling preacher for inland missions."

This teacher turned preacher was the Reverend Tamme Vanden Bosch, nephew of our first minister. With his wife he posed for a picture as he was ready to begin his new work. The dominie was seated in a chair and in the custom of that day, his wife stood obediently behind him, with her hand on his shoulder and her long full skirts touching the floor.

The traveling preacher began his work at Clam Union, now Vogel Center, in the lumberland of northern Michigan. The church paid him five hundred fifty dollars a year for his work, and once he gave back a hundred dollars to start a fund for giving Bibles to people who needed them.

There were other early home missionaries, willing to travel from state to state, from settlement to settlement, in prairie schooner and lumber wagon, through snow and storm, sometimes lost, often tired, but always ready to move on wherever new groups of settlers could be gathered into a church. For years, as long as the ships brought immigrants and as long as Dutch-Americans moved to new places, this bringing in of churches went on, especially west of the Mississippi River. In 1947 it began all over again in Canada when Dutch settlers poured into that country after the second world war. Through home missionaries, speaking Dutch and English, most of our Canadian churches were established.

Today this kind of home mission work, which we call church extension, still continues. But we are also beginning the other kind of home mission work — speaking to our neighbors who are not Dutch and who do not believe on the Lord Jesus Christ.

For the sixty years that we spoke the Dutch language we were not ready to talk to our American neighbors. When their language became ours, we still had many questions about witnessing to the people next door. We did not think they would be interested in our church or in what we believe. We did not know how to talk to them even if they were interested. And we thought that perhaps we could not stay pure and faithful to our beliefs if we took into our churches people who had not grown up in them. In our hearts we were still a church walled-in.

But there were beginnings. Here and there a church began a mission in another part of its own city. The earliest of these city mission was in Chicago just before the first world war, and many churches have started city missions and neighborhood chapels of their own since that time. We have set up missions in Paterson and Chicago for our Jewish neighbors, of whom Jesus said that some will accept him as the true Messiah and be saved. Much later we began to work with our Negro neighbors in the Harlem section of New York City. Here we were glad to have our first Negro minister in charge. We gave thanks also for the two Chinese-American seminary graduates of our church who began the work with Chinese-American students and families in New York City and Chicago.

In 1939 the Christian Reformed Church went on the air. It was our first voice as a church to the American people of our great home mission field. The tremendous response to the Back to God Hour has answered some of our questions and taken away some of our excuses. It proves beyond a doubt that we have been given a faith and life which America needs. It proves that we can speak of this faith in a way our neighbors understand, without leaving out parts of it or watering it down. And if our faith can be shared, then something is wrong with us if we cannot share our church also.

This sharing is still new to us, though Christ spoke of it almost two thousand years ago. The work to be done is frightening because it is so big. It gives us a huge new mission field and places each one of us right in the middle of it. We all become missionaries instead of only paying and praying for others to do the work far away. Every one of our churches becomes a church of Christ for all kinds of Americans, not only for "our own" Dutch but for Christ's own of every background.

There are problems in this new mission field, just as our missionaries in Africa and Japan tell us they have problems where they work. Our problems at home are different, because the people around us often call themselves Christians and they are satisfied with their comfortable way of living.

But the problems do not stop the work in our new mission field. They only make us work harder, with more patience, more love, more prayer. There is no change in what we believe, only in what we do with what we believe.

We have some trail-blazing churches in this work. They are

churches where outsiders have become insiders, where the praying and the giving and the working is wonderful to see. Such churches have not been built in a day, but slowly and surely they are becoming strong. Arcadia, Monsey, Lakewood City, Salt Lake City, Albuquerque, Oklahoma City, Columbus, and Harlem are some of them.

Year by year others of our churches wake up to see the blocks of homes around them for the first time. They find they do not even need to go across the tracks or to the other side of the city to work with their neighbors because their first neighbors are within the shadow of their church buildings. Children invite their playmates to Sunday School and Vacation Bible School. Parents bring their neighbors with them to special events at the church and show them Christian friendship in many ways. Everyone welcomes strangers at a Sunday service.

This is the new frontier of the Christian Reformed Church. It can be found wherever we are ready to look for it. It is all around us.

In all the centuries of the church of Christ, God has raised up men at special times to do his work. So also he prepares churches. He blesses them and then lays a challenge before them.

In the mighty land of America, among the true churches of Christ, there is a small church which God has been preparing and blessing. Today he lays a challenge before it.

Speak, says God to the church called Christian Reformed. Speak for me to the people of America. Go on speaking far away in Africa and the Orient, but speak now also to the neighbors whose homes are next to your own. And while you speak and work, hold fast to the truth, which is my Word.

So I will be with you and bless you, and make you to be a blessing. Through you also I will build my church.

190

IN APPRECIATION

I have not written this book without help which I appreciate deeply.

To Dr. Henry Zylstra I am especially indebted. The idea of the book was born in his mind, and with his early encouragement and continued helpfulness the book has been completed. I have appreciated also the valuable suggestions of Dr. John Kromminga, President of Calvin Seminary, who read the manuscript.

And there are others whom I do not thank by name — missionaries, ministers, staff members in the offices of the Back to God Hour and the Board of Missions, my publisher, and members of my family. One does not write a book, particularly a first book, without help such as this.

Above all, God is to be thanked and praised. In his love and through his Son, he has made possible the true story which this book tries to tell.

T. V. H.

The drawings on pages 60, 65, 66, 67, 69, 71 and 72 appeared originally in *Holland's Heritage Portfolio* and are used by kind permission of the First National Bank of Holland, Michigan. Those on pages 61, 70, 87, 98 and 175 are used by kind permission of the Centennial Committee of the Christian Reformed Church. All of the drawings are by Dirk Gringhuis.